Everett and Gleason

Catalogue and Retail Price-List of Vegetable and Flower Seeds

Everett and Gleason

Catalogue and Retail Price-List of Vegetable and Flower Seeds

ISBN/EAN: 9783742812155

Manufactured in Europe, USA, Canada, Australia, Japa

Cover: Foto ©Gila Hanssen / pixelio.de

Manufactured and distributed by brebook publishing software
(www.brebook.com)

Everett and Gleason

Catalogue and Retail Price-List of Vegetable and Flower Seeds

CATALOGUE

AND

RETAIL PRICE-LIST

OF

VEGETABLE AND FLOWER

SEEDS,

HERB, TREE, AND GRASS SEEDS,

SEED GRAIN, AND BIRD SEEDS,

FLOWER ROOTS, &C.

OFFERED FOR SALE BY

EVERETT & GLEASON,

Importers and Wholesale and Retail Dealers in

AMERICAN &? FOREIGN GARDEN &? AGRICULTURAL SEEDS,

WAREHOUSE, **34** SOUTH MARKET ST.,

BOSTON, MASS.

TO PURCHASERS

IT gives us pleasure to present herewith our Catalogue and general Retail Price-List of Garden, Agricultural, and other Seeds. We ask for it your kind attention, and hope that on looking it through you will notice many varieties of Seeds you need, find our prices satisfactory, and be pleased to favor us with your orders.

Our Stock is excellent in every respect; the varieties the choicest and best in cultivation; and having been carefully grown, for the most part, from our own stocks, and those of our growers having our approval, we do not hesitate to express our belief that no better or more reliable stock is to be found in this country.

We invite particular attention to our lists of Vegetables and Flowers, which, freed from the incumbrance of undesirable sorts, are much easier to make selections from than from longer lists where poor and worthless varieties are intermingled with the good and valuable. The varieties of Vegetables have been selected for their general excellence and profit, suited alike for Market Gardeners' and Family uses; the Flowers as the most ornamental and beautiful, adapted to the wants of Florists, Amateurs, and Home Culture generally.

Selection of Seeds. In the selection of Seeds, we beg to remind purchasers of the very great importance of their selecting only the choicest and best to be obtained, as from these only can the most satisfactory returns be expected. Seeds grown from stock not properly selected, and without proper attention during and after their growth, in order to make them *Low-Priced* or *Cheap*, are unsafe to touch, and should never be used when reliable Seeds are possible to obtain. The result of using the *best* is satisfaction and profit; the use of the *cheap* (in by far the majority of cases) is dissatisfaction and loss. The extra care and attention required to produce the *best*, necessarily entails slightly advanced prices over the cost of the common, but these are largely overbalanced and repaid by the increased value of the crop.

About Warranting. Notwithstanding the greatest care is taken by us to have all our Seeds of the best quality, we do not warrant them, and this because of failures that are liable to occur, over which we have no control, and which we cannot be responsible for, such as imperfect planting, unsuitable condition of the soil (either too dry, cold, or wet), workings of worms and insects, too hot manures, botanical changes of crossed varieties, etc., either of which are quite possible to occur, while at the same time it would be utterly impossible for us to account for the occurrence, and thus failures arise through no fault on our part. We therefore wish it distinctly understood that Seeds sold by us WE DO NOT WARRANT IN ANY RESPECT, and sales will not be made except on this condition. At the same time we shall not sell, or allow to be sold from our store, Seeds of any kind or quality attached to which is a doubt that they are otherwise than as we recommend them, or that we would not plant if they were required for our own use.

TERMS:

Our Terms are Net Cash. All Bills on which short credits are allowed are due the first of the month succeeding the date of purchase. Bills on which longer time is desired must be provided for by special agreement.

Our Prices. We have made our prices as low as Seeds of the same quality can be afforded, and shall adhere to present quotations as closely as possible; but should a scarcity, or other condition of the market, necessitate changes, we reserve the right to make such changes without notice. Our customers may be assured, however, that we shall as readily accord them the benefit of all reductions, as any advances we may be compelled to make. All quotations, we wish it understood, are for the *best* quality of the variety quoted, unless otherwise specially mentioned.

Varieties, particularly Clover and Grass Seeds, Bird Seeds, Onion Sets, and Seed Potatoes, in which fluctuations of prices are quite likely to occur, and which are not quoted, will be furnished at the market rate (for goods of like quality) at the time orders are filled.

Orders. Orders from known correspondents (cash or accepted credit) will at all times receive our careful and prompt attention. Orders from *unknown* correspondents will receive equal attention *if accompanied by a remittance for the amount of the order, or satisfactory references.*

Remittances. Remittances may be made by Post Office Money Order, Bank Draft, Registered Letter, or for amounts less than Two Dollars, in Bank Bills, at our risk. For fractional parts of a dollar, postage stamps may be sent.

Seeds by Mail. As Seeds can be sent by Mail to all parts of the United States, at the rate of ONE CENT FOR EACH OUNCE, no person who wishes our Seeds need be without them (see our remarks on *Orders* and *Remittances* above, and write for what is wanted.) We send all Seeds ordered at *Ounce* or *Packet* prices, FREE. Seeds at *Pound* prices, and Peas, Beans, Corn, Clover Seed, Seed Grain, Roots, etc., we do not send free, as these are quoted at *net* prices at store. Purchasers desiring these by mail are requested to remit an additional amount sufficient to cover the postage, at the rate of SIXTEEN CENTS PER POUND, or THIRTY CENTS PER QUART. Particular attention is invited to this, as, when omitted, the amount will be deducted from that received.

Address, etc. Persons ordering Seeds by mail are requested to be particular to write their OWN NAME, and also the names of their TOWN, POST OFFICE, COUNTY and STATE, plainly, and NOT TO OMIT EITHER, as serious delays are occasioned by such omissions. If Seeds ordered are not received within a reasonable time thereafter, notice should be sent us, so that the delay may be accounted for and remedied at once.

Bags Used in Packing. Clover and Grass Seed Bags, and Bird Seed Sacks, are not returnable. Others sent out on general Seed orders, at our regular prices, will be received at the same rates if returned *sound and in good condition*, within *thirty days* from date of sale. THIS AGREEMENT IS VOID IF THE BAGS ARE USED FOR OTHER PURPOSES BEFORE RETURNING. MEALY BAGS ARE NOT RECEIVED AT ANY PRICE.

BAGS ARE FURNISHED AT THE FOLLOWING RATES:

Quarter-Bushel, best quality, 10 cents.   One-Bushel, best quality, 20 cents.
Half-Bushel,   "   "   15 "   Two-Bushel,   "   "   25 "

Parties *remitting* with their orders will please include in their remittance the requisite amount for bags.

SPECIAL LIST
OF
VEGETABLE SEEDS.

This list comprises recently introduced varieties, some quite new, and others older, of which brief descriptions are given.

BEAN. TALL TRANSYLVANIAN BUTTER.

A new running variety from Germany, described as robust growing, excellent and productive, with very long, broad, fleshy, and stringless pods.

Per Packet, 15 cents.

BEAN. DWARF GOLDEN WAX.

Not new, but until recently its merits were comparatively unknown. It is a most excellent variety, either for Market Gardeners' or Family use. It is the earliest and most prolific of the Dwarf Wax-Pod sorts, producing larger pods, creamy white in color, which are very tender, stringless, and fine flavored. It is also good for green shelling, and as a dry Bean for later use.

Per Packet, 10 cts. | Per Quart, 30 cts. | Per Bushel, $7.00.

BEAN. YELLOW ETAMPES SOJA.

Of the Soja sorts this is the best for culinary purposes, having a fine flavor, cooks well, and is very nutritious. It is used and cooked the same as other Beans, either green or dry. The plant grows about twenty inches high, and yields enormously. It is also useful for fodder for stock.

Per Packet, 15 cents.

CABBAGE. VERY EARLY ETAMPES.

A new French variety, recommended as the best of all early varieties.

Per Packet, 15 cents.

CABBAGE. LITTLE PIXIE.

Not new, but a very excellent and very early variety, heads very hard, and good in quality. Fine for Marketing and for Family use.

Per Packet, 10 cts. | Per Ounce, 25 cts.

CELERY. CRAWFORD'S HALF DWARF.

This variety is grown very extensively by the Market Gardeners around New York, who give it the preference to all other varieties. It blanches well, is very solid, has a fine nutty flavor, and is a good and vigorous grower. It does not tiller or have side shoots like the Boston Market variety, and by some is preferred on that account.

Per Packet, 15 cents. | Per Ounce, 50 cents.

CELERY. GOLDEN DWARF.

A very distinct variety, also largely grown by the Market Gardeners around New York city for that market. In size and habit it is much like the other Half Dwarf kinds, except that when blanched, the heart, which is large and full, is of a waxy, golden yellow, rendering it a most striking and showy variety. It is very solid, of most excellent flavor, and one of the very best keepers during winter known.

Per Packet, 15 cents. | Per Ounce, 60 cents.

CORN. EXTRA EARLY MARBLEHEAD SWEET.

This is an eight-rowed, flesh-colored, very early variety ; claimed by the introducer to be fully a week earlier than any of the early sweet varieties at present in use. The plant is of dwarf habit ; ears of medium size, and set low down on the stalk.

Per Packet, 15 cts. | Per Quart, 40 cts. | Per Peck, $2.00.

CORN. MARBLEHEAD MAMMOTH SWEET.

This is an excellent sort for family use or for marketing, very sweet, and is the earliest of the *large* varieties, a very valuable quality, as most of the *large* varieties are late. The ears are very large, and have been found to weigh, fresh from the stalk, two and three pounds each.

Per Packet, 10 cts. | Per Peck, $1.50.

CUCUMBER. WHITE SPINE. (For Forcing.)

This is a very choice selection of the true Early White Spine variety, so largely grown under glass during winter, for the Boston market. It is not only excellent in quality, but is also the most profitable variety for winter forcing that has thus far been introduced, yielding in experienced hands, with best culture, immense crops.

Per Packet, 10 cts. | Per Ounce, 25 cts. | Per Pound, $3.00.

DANDELION. PARIS VERY EARLY.

A new variety of French Dandelion, recommended as making a very early growth ; especially suitable for Market Gardeners, and forcing under glass.

Per Packet, 10 cents. | Per Ounce, 75 cents.

MUSKMELON. IMPROVED HACKENSACK.

An exceedingly fine Melon in every respect ; of good size, round, flattened at the ends, skin green, and roughly netted ; flesh green, sweet, rich and delicious. A splendid variety either for Marketing or for Family use.

Per Packet, 5 cts. | Per Ounce, 15 cts. | Per Pound, $1.50.

MELON. SURPRISE.

A very excellent variety, recently introduced. It has a thin cream-colored skin, thickly netted ; the flesh is of a deep salmon color, very thick, and of exquisite flavor. It is also a good bearer, is round in shape, and of good size.

Per Packet, 10 cts. | Per Ounce, 20 cts. | Per Pound, $1.50.

ONION. DANVERS THICK YELLOW.

We have no new variety under this title to offer, but we wish to ask special attention to the very excellent stock of this kind offered in our general list. It is conceded by the best onion growers for the Boston market, that no seed grown gives better or more satisfactory results than the *true Buxton* stock as selected by Mr. Buxton for many years past. We offer seed of his own growing, and also seed grown from his stock by one of our best growers.

Price, see page 13. Special Prices on application, if wanted in quantity.

PEA. AMERICAN WONDER.

This new and excellent variety is a seedling, the result of a cross between the favorite and well known sorts, **Champion of England and Little Gem.** It combines all the good qualities of both its parents, with the additional ones of superiority in flavor to the Champion, and of greater productiveness than the Little Gem, besides being earlier than any of the wrinkled varieties. Planted on good soil, each vine will average twelve pods, and each pod six peas. The vine grows from eight to twelve inches high, and on good soil, if not planted too thickly, branches at the joints, forming little bushes, literally covered and almost hidden with pods. In planting, to obtain the best results, the rows should be much closer than for the general varieties of Early Peas, and the Peas should be more thinly or sparsely distributed in the rows. Good soil, not too dry, suits them best.

Per Packet, 20 cts. | Per Quart, 75 cts. | Per Peck, $5.00.

PEA. TELEPHONE.

This is a new English variety, and is said to have won more prizes than any other Pea of modern introduction. It is a green wrinkled sort, pods long and large, containing nine to eleven peas, which are of exquisite sugary flavor. Vines are of medium height, and yield enormously.

Per Packet, 15 cts. | Per Quart, 50 cts.

SQUASH. COCOANUT.

This is a small-sized, ornamental, as well as useful variety, being creamy white in color, with a spot of deep green on the blossom end about three inches in diameter. It is very prolific, and the Squashes are fine grained, very sweet, and rich flavored.

Per Packet, 10 cts. | Per Ounce, 25 cts.

SQUASH. PERFECT GEM.

An excellent variety, equally desirable either as a summer or winter variety. As long keepers, we have kept them a year in fine condition. The vine is a strong grower, and has been known to yield as many as twenty Squashes on a single vine. The Squashes are round, four to six inches in diameter, creamy white in color, and dry, sweet and rich flavored when cooked.

Per Packet, 10 cts. | Per Ounce, 25 cts.

SPINACH. LONG STANDING.

A new variety, with thick dark green leaves and compact growth. Recommended as three weeks later in running to seed than other sorts — a quality greatly desired, and gives in this variety a special value, particularly to Market Gardeners.

Per Ounce, 10 cts. | Per Pound, 60 cts.

TOMATO. EARLY ALPHA.

Probably the earliest variety in cultivation; fruit of bright red color, generally smooth, sometimes slightly ribbed; ripens well, seldom cracks; solid, fine flavored, and produces abundantly.

Per Packet, 15 cents.

TOMATO. ESSEX HYBRID.

It is claimed by the introducer of this variety, and seems to be sustained by tests, that this is the handsomest shaped and most profitable Tomato for the market in cultivation, and will bear more marketable fruit than any other variety. It is very early, solid, rich-flavored, large in size, grows perfectly smooth, of a bright pink color, and is extremely productive. It possesses more of the important qualities of a perfect Tomato than any other known sort. It ripens all over alike, leaving no green spots around the stem, so objectionable in some other varieties. It is fine for growing under glass, the fruits being uniformly of the best quality. TRY IT.

Per Packet, 10 cts. | Per Ounce, 60 cts.

TOMATO. "MAYFLOWER."

This new variety, introduced from Vermont, is recommended as the *earliest large* Tomato cultivated, ripening but a few days later than the very early variety, "Little Gem," and averaging in size about one third larger than "Acme." It is of a glossy, bright red color, so desirable in a market Tomato, and ripens as evenly and perfectly up to the stem that it presents a most beautiful appearance. Its shape is perfect, globular, slightly flattened, and perfectly smooth; flesh solid, unusually free from seeds, and of rich, excellent flavor. In productiveness it is not excelled by any other sort, and is an excellent shipper, bearing a large amount of handling without injury.

Per Packet, 25 cents.

TOMATO. LIVINGSTON'S PERFECTION.

This variety is described by its originator as the largest early sort known, of blood-red color, perfectly smooth, with few seeds, ripens all over and through at the same time, a good shipper, and for canning purposes is not excelled by any other. It is larger than Acme, and earlier than Acme or Paragon.

Per Packet, 15 cts. | Per Ounce, 50 cts.

TOMATO. PRESIDENT GARFIELD.

A new variety, originating in Servia, and described as of very luxuriant growth and extraordinary fertility. The plants attain a large size and require plenty of room. The fruits are of enormous size (weighing from two to three pounds in full-grown specimens), ripen quite evenly, have but few seeds, are very solid, with beautiful tender flesh, the flavor of which is delicious.

Per Packet, 25 cents.

TURNIP. VERY EARLY PURPLE-TOP MUNICH.

A new flat-shaped variety, with white flesh, skin white under ground and purple red above. Its special value consists in its earliness, which is remarkable, being two to three weeks earlier than any other variety, a quality which admits of much later fall sowing with certainty of crop than the common fall sorts, as well as useful for very early crops.

Per Packet, 10 cents. | Per Ounce, 30 cents.

BLUNT'S PROLIFIC CORN.

FOR ENSILAGE.

After another year's trial of this corn for ensilage purposes, we can confidently state that it has given very great satisfaction wherever used, yielding immense crops of forage of the best quality. Bearing in its general appearance so close a resemblance to the Southern White Flat or Dent Corn, purchasers are liable to be mislead and purchase the latter, as it sells for a much less price; consequently those who have had the misfortune to fall into this error are unable to appreciate its superiority over the common varieties; once, however, the true is had, the difference is seen at once. If not planted too thickly, it attains in good soil a height of twelve to fifteen feet. The quantity of seed required per acre, to secure the best results, remains undetermined as yet, the quantities so far used ranging from half a bushel to one and a half, and in some cases two bushels, to the acre. Nearly all growers approve of rows three feet apart; but *in the row* some prefer sowing thickly, while others prefer the plants to stand six inches apart, thereby gaining more healthy leafage and stronger plants, that will stand against wind.

Per Bushel, $2.50.

RUSSIAN WHITE OATS.

The Russian White Oats are prolific without parallel, yielding with ordinary cultivation one hundred bushels per acre. They are now being tested in nearly every State of the Union, and the reports thus far are unanimous in commending them as the heaviest yielding variety at present known. They are extremely hardy, enduring the coldest climate in our country without injury, and are absolutely rust proof. They tiller wonderfully; from twenty-five to forty stalks are produced from a single seed, the heads of grain measuring from sixteen to twenty-two inches in length. The straw is large, and strong enough to support these enormous heads. The grain is heavy and the chaff light, so that a *measured* bushel weighs considerably more than a bushel of ordinary oats. The variety, without doubt, is destined when more widely known, to become the standard sort.

Per Bushel, $2.00.

EVERETT & GLEASON'S

RETAIL PRICE-LIST

Vegetable 🌿 Agricultural Seeds.

→✳ 1882 ✳←

In the following lists, it has not so much been our purpose to offer the largest number of varieties, as to offer those select varieties that have proved most valuable, and can be depended on to give a satisfactory return when properly treated. Of their good quality we desire to give the most ample assurance that our best efforts have been devoted to their careful selection, to the end that they may prove reliable, and what they purport to be. The preservation of the purity and excellence of the stock the home-grown varieties have been produced from has received our particular attention, and in the selection of the foreign varieties our best judgment has been exercised.

☞ **PRICES.** Our prices are quoted by Weight, per Ounce and Pound; and by Measure, per Quart and Bushel.

By Weight; Quantities LESS than four Ounces, we sell at the OUNCE RATE. Quantities of FOUR OUNCES and upwards are sold at the POUND RATE.

By Measure; we sell Quantities LESS than FOUR QUARTS at the QUART RATE. Quantities more than FOUR QUARTS at the BUSHEL RATE.

For varieties required in larger quantities, special prices will be given on application.

PEAS—(Pisum Sativum).	pr pkt.	per qt.	per bush.
French, *Pois*. Spanish, *Guissante*. German, *Erbse*.			
Early Kentish Invicta, the best first early (Imported)	.10	.40	8.00
Early Kentish Invicta, " " " " (American)	.10	.40	7.00
Extra Early (selected Podded Stock)	.10	.40	7.00
Early Caractacus (Imported)	.10	.40	8.00
Early Dexter (American)	.10	.30	6.50
Early Daniel O'Rourke (American), extra selected	.10	.30	6.50
Philadelphia Extra Early	.10	.30	6.50
Carter's First Crop (Imported)	.10	.40	8.00
Early Tom Thumb (American)	.10	.40	7.00
American Wonder (green wrinkled, very dwarf)	.20	.75	20.00
Laxton's Alpha	10	.40	7 00
McLean's Little Gem	.10	.40	8.00
Carter's Premium Gem	.10	.40	9.00
McLean's Advancer, (Choice Stock)	.10	.40	7.00
McLean's Advancer, (Extra Selected Podded Stock)	.10	.40	8.00
Champion of England (American)	.10	.30	6.00
Champion of England (Imported)			
Yorkshire Hero	.10	.40	8.00
Blue Imperial	.10	.30	6.00
Dwarf Large White Marrow (best Marrow, extra)	.10	.20	3.50
Black Eye Marrow (selected stock)	.10	.20	3.00
Sugar, or String (eatable pods)	.15	.50	12.00

BEANS—Dwarf or Bush.

French, Haricots Nains. Spanish, *Habichuelas Enanas.*
German, *Busch Bohne.*

	pr pkt.	per qt.	per bush.
Early Fejee	.10	.30	5.00
Early Rachel	.10	.30	5.00
Early China	.10	.30	5.00
Early Long Yellow	.10	.30	5.00
Early Mohawk	.10	.30	5.00
Dwarf Horticultural	.10	.30	6.00
Early White Wax (Yellow Pod)	.10	.30	6.00
Dwarf Black Wax (Yellow Pod)	.10	.30	6.00
Dwarf Golden Wax (Yellow Pod)	.10	.30	7.00
Early Valentine	.10	.30	5.00
Refugee (Pickling Bean)	.10	.30	5.00
Dwarf Yellow Cranberry	.10	.30	7.00
Large White Marrow	.10	.20	4.50
Long White Kidney	.10	.20	4.50
White Pea (true early, even ripening variety)	.10	.20	4.50
Turtle Soup	.10	.20	4.50

BEANS—English (Faba Vulgaris).

French, Feve de Marais. Spanish, *Haba Inglis.*
German, *Grosse Englische Bohne.*

	pr pkt.	per qt.	per bush.
Broad Windsor	.10	.30	8.00
Mazagan	.10	.30	7.00

BEANS—Pole or Running.

French, Haricots a Rames. Spanish, *Judios.*
German, *Stangen Bohne.*

	pr pkt.	per qt.	per bush.
Large White Lima	.10	.40	10.00
Dreer's Improved Lima	.10	.40	11.00
Sieva, or Small Lima	.10	.40	8.00
Pole Horticultural	.10	.30	6.00
Red Cranberry	.10	.30	8.00
White Caseknife	.10	.30	7.00
Indian Chief (Yellow Pod)	.10	.30	7.00
Pole White Wax (Yellow Pod)	.10	.40	8.00
Red Giant Wax (Yellow Pod)	.10	.40	10.00
Concord	.10	.30	7.00
Scarlet Runner	.10	.40	8.00
White Runner	.10	.40	8.00

CORN—Garden Sweet, or Sugar.

French, *Sucre Mais*. Spanish, *Azucar Maiz*.
German, *Zucker Mais*.

	pr pkt.	per qt.	per bush.
Marblehead Extra Early (eight-rowed)	.15	.40	8.00
Extra Early Tom Thumb (eight-rowed)	.10	.25	5.00
Extra Early Minnesota (eight-rowed)	.10	.25	4.00
Extra Early Narragansett (eight-rowed)	.10	.25	4.00
Early Crosby (twelve-rowed) Boston Market variety	.10	.25	5.00
Moore's Concord (twelve to sixteen-rowed)	.10	.25	4.00
Burr's Mammoth (twelve to sixteen-rowed)	.10	.25	4.00
Stowell's Evergreen (twelve to sixteen-rowed)	.10	.25	4.00
Potter's Excelsior (eight-rowed, very sweet)	.10	.25	5.00
Black Mexican (eight-rowed)	.10	.25	5.00
Fodder Sweet (for Soiling)			2.50

CORN—Indian, or Flint (Zea Mays).

French, *Mais*. Spanish, *Maiz*. German, *Welschkorn*.

	pr ear.	per qt.	per bush.
Early Yellow Canada (eight-rowed)	3	.15	2.50
Large Yellow (eight-rowed)	3	.15	2.50

POPPING CORN.

White (Selected Ears for Seed)	5

ASPARAGUS—(Asparagus Officinalis).

French, *Asperge*. Spanish, *Esparrago*. German, *Spargel*.

	pr pkt.	per oz.	per lb.
Giant, Purple Top (selected stock)	5	.10	1.00
Conover's Colossal	5	.10	.75
Moore's Giant (very large, extra)	5	.15	1.50

ASPARAGUS ROOTS.

	per hund. 1 year.	per hund. 2 years	per thous.
Moore's Giant	.60	1.00	
Colossal	.60	1.00	

ARTICHOKE—(Cynara Scolymus).

French, *Artichaut*. Spanish, *Alcachofa*.
German, *Artischoke*.

	pr pkt.	per oz.	per lb.
French Green Globe	5	.30	3.00

BEET—(Beta Vulgaris).

French, *Betterave*. Spanish, *Remolacha*.
German, *Runkelrube*.

	pr pkt.	per oz.	per lb.
Egyptian Early Turnip Rooted (extra early)	5	.15	1.50
Bastian's Early Turnip Blood (fine early)	5	.10	.60
Dewing's Early Turnip Blood (Market Stock, extra)	5	.10	.60
Dewing's Early Turnip Blood (very good stock)	5	.10	.50
Early Bassano, Turnip Rooted	5	.10	.60
Early Turnip Blood (for greens)	—	—	.35
Early Yellow, Turnip Rooted	5	.10	.80
Long Smooth Blood (American)	5	.10	.60
Swiss Chard (for greens)	5	.10	.80
White Silesian Sugar	5	.10	.40
Mangel Wurzel, Long Red	5	.10	.40
—— —— Giant Long Red	5	.10	.40
—— —— Ovoid Yellow	5	.10	.40
—— —— Yellow Globe	5	.10	.40

BORECOLE. See Kale.

BROCOLI—(Brassica Oleracea Botrytis).

French, *Chou Brocoli*. Spanish, *Broculi*.
German, *Spargel Kohl*.

	pr pkt.	per oz.	per lb.
Early White Walcheren	.10	.60	8.00
Large Purple Cape	.10	.50	5.00

BRUSSELS SPROUTS—
(Brassica Oleracea, var).

French, *Chou de Bruxelles*. Spanish, *Breton d'Brusselas*.

	pr pkt.	per oz.	per lb.
Dwarf Improved French	.10	.20	2.50
English	.10	.20	2.50

CAULIFLOWER—
(Brassica Oleracea Botrytis).

French, *Choufleur*. Spanish, *Coliflor*. German, *Blumen Kohl*.

	pr pkt.	per oz.	per lb.
Extra Early Dwarf Erfurt (very fine)	.25	2.00	24.00
Early Extra Snowball (most excellent and profitable)	.50	5.00	—
Half-Early Paris (extra)	.10	.75	10.00
Lenormand (short stemmed)	.10	.75	10.00
Veitch's Autumn Giant	.10	.75	10.00
Algiers (very large, fine heading)	.10	.75	10.00

CABBAGE—(Brassica Oleracea Capitata).

French, *Chou Cabus*. Spanish, *Repollo*. German, *Kopf-Kohl*.

	pr pkt.	per oz.	per lb.
Early Wyman (Large Early)			
Early Jersey Wakefield (extra)	.10	.40	6.00
Henderson's Early Summer	.10	.40	6.00
Early York	5	.20	2.00
Early Large Ox-Heart	5	.20	2.00
Early Sugarloaf	5	.20	2.00
Winnigstadt (Pointed Head)	5	.20	2.00
Improved Brunswick (extra)	5	.40	4.00
Flat Dutch Drumhead (American, fine)	5	.25	3.00
Stone-Mason Drumhead (extra)	.10	.40	4.00
Marblehead Mammoth (very large)	5	.40	4.00
Globe Curled Savoy (American, extra Market Stock)	5	.40	4.00
Drumhead Savoy (cross of Drumhead and Globe Savoy)	5	.30	3.00
English Curled Savoy (for greens)		.10	.75
Large Red Drumhead (extra)	5	.40	4.00

CARROT—(Daucus Carota).

French, *Carotte*. Spanish, *Zanahoria*. German, *Mohre*.

	pr pkt.	per oz.	per lb.
Early Scarlet Forcing	5	.20	2.00
Early Scarlet Horn, or Butter	5	.15	1.50
Danvers Half-Long Orange	5	.15	1.50
Thick Half-Long Orange	5	.10	1.25
Long Orange	5	.10	.80
Long White Belgian	5	.10	.80

CELERY—(Apium Graveolens).

French, *Celeri*. Spanish, *Apio* German, *Seleri*.

	pr pkt.	per oz.	per lb.
Boston Market Dwarf White	.10	.40	5.00
Sandringham Dwarf White	5	.30	3.00
Carter's Crimson	5	.30	3.00
Celery Seed (for flavoring)		5	.40

CELERIAC—or Turnip-Rooted Celery.

French, *Celeri Rave*. Spanish, *Seleri*.
German, *Knoll oder Kopf*.

	pr pkt.	per oz.	per lb.
Apple-Shaped (extra)	5	.25	2.50

CHERVIL — (Scandix Cerefolium).

French, *Cerfeuil.* Spanish, *Perefollo.* German, *Korbel.*

	pr pkt.	per oz.	per lb.
Curled	5	.20	2.00

CHICORY — (Cichorium Intybus).

French, *Chicoree.* Spanish, *Sauvage a gros Racine.*
German, *Chichorien Wurzel.*

	pr pkt.	per oz.	per lb.
Coffee, or Large-Rooted	5	.15	1.50

CIVES — (Allium Schoenoprasum).

French, *Ciboulette.* Spanish, *Cebollina.*
German, *Schnitt-Lauch.*

	pr pkt.	per oz.	per lb.
Garden Cives	.25		

CORN. See page seventh of this list.

CORN SALAD — (Valeriana Locusta).

French, *Mache.* Spanish, *Canoniga.* German, *Ackersalat.*

	pr pkt.	per oz.	per lb.
Round-Leaved	5	.10	1.00

CUCUMBER — (Cucumis Sativus).

French, *Concombre.* Spanish, *Pepino.* German, *Gurke.*

	pr pkt.	per oz.	per lb.
Extra Early Russian	5	.10	.80
Early Cluster	5	.10	.80
White Spined (fine for hot beds and marketing)	5	.10	.80
Early Short Green or Frame	5	.10	.80
Long Prickly	5	.10	.80
London Long Green	5	.10	.80
Long White (pure white)	.10	.25	2.50
Boston Pickling (American Gherkin)	5	.10	.80
Green Prolific (pickling)	5	.10	.80
West India Gherkin (Burr Cucumber)	.10	.25	2.50

ENGLISH (Long Sorts for Forcing).

Rollison's Telegraph	.35		
Blue Gown	.35		
Daniel's Duke of Edinburgh	.35		
Marquis of Lorne	.50		

CRESS — (Lepidium Sativum).

French, *Cresson.* Spanish, *Mastuerzo.* German, *Kresse.*

	pr pkt.	per oz.	per lb.
Curled, or Peppergrass	5	.10	.80
Water Cress (Nasturtium Officinalis)	.10	.40	4.00

DANDELION — (Taraxacum Dens-Leonis).

French, *Dent de Lion.* Spanish, *Amargon.*
German, *Lewengohn.*

	pr pkt.	per oz.	per lb.
French Thick-Leaved (Imported, true)	.10	.30	4.00
French Thick-Leaved (American, Market Stock Extra)	.10	.40	5.00
Paris, very early, *new*	.10	.75	

EGG PLANT — (Solanum Melongena).

French, *Aubergine.* Spanish, *Berengena.*
German, *Eierpflange.*

	pr pkt.	per oz.	per lb.
Very Early Dwarf Purple	.10	.40	4.00
Early Long Purple	.10	.40	4.00
Large Oval Purple (very large)	.10	.50	6.00
Black Pekin (extra fine)	.15	.60	8.00

ENDIVE — (Chicorium Endive).

French, *Chicoree.* Spanish, *Endivia.* German, *Endivien.*

	pr pkt.	per oz.	per lb.
Green Curled	5	.20	2.00
Broad-Leaved Batavian (Scarolle)	5	.20	2.00

KOHL RABI — (Brassica Caulo-Rapa).

French, *Chou Rave.* Spanish, *Colinabo.*
German, *Kohl Rabi uber der erde.*

	pr pkt.	per oz.	per lb.
Early White Vienna (short-leaved, very early)	5	.25	3.00
Earliest Green Erfurt (excellent open-ground sort)	5	.25	3.00
Giant White	.10	.40	4.00
Giant Purple	.10	.40	4.00

KALE, or Borecole.

French, *Chou frise vert a pied court.* Spanish, *Breton.*
German, *Blatter Kohl.*

	pr pkt.	per oz.	per lb.
Dwarf Green Curled (German greens)	5	.10	1.00

LEEK — (Allium Porrum).

French, *Poireau.* Spanish, *Puerro.* German, *Lauch.*

	pr pkt.	per oz.	per lb.
Erfurt Winter Flag	5	.20	2.00
Musselburg Broad Flag (Best American)	5	.25	3.00
Mammoth Flag	.10	.40	4.00

LETTUCE—(Lactuca Sativa).

French, *Laitue.* Spanish, *Lechuga.* German, *Lattich Salat.*

	pr pkt.	per oz.	per lb.
Boston Fine Curled (black seed), Market Stock, extra.....	—	—	—
Boston Fine Curled (black seed), of the trade	5	.20	2.50
Early Curled Simpson (fine for early cutting)............	5	.20	2.50
Black-Seeded Tennisball (Market Stock, extra)	5	.40	4.00
Black-Seeded Tennisball, of the trade	5	.20	250
White-Seeded Tennisball, or Boston Market Head (for culture under glass), extra selected stock....	.10	.40	5.00
White-Seeded Tennisball, of the trade.............	5	.20	2.50
Princess Head (very fine)	5	.30	3.00
All the Year Round (fine).............................	5	.30	3.00
Hanson	5	.30	3.00
Summer Cabbage	5	.20	2.50
India Head...	5	.30	300
Perpignan (remains long in head)	5	.30	3.00
White Paris Cos (Romaine)	5	.30	3.00

MARTYNIA—(Martynia Proboscidia).

	pr pkt.	per oz.	per lb.
Pickling Martynia	5	.30	3.00

MELON, Watermelon—(Cucurbita Citrullus).

French, *Melon d'Eau.* Spanish, *Melon de agua ó Zandia.* German, *Wassermelone.*

	pr pkt.	per oz.	per lb.
Vick's Early (extra)................................	5	.15	1.50
Phinney's Early	5	.10	.80
Mountain Sweet (fine)	5	.10	.80
Black Spanish (sweet, very fine).....................	5	.10	.80
Orange.............................	5	.10	1.00
Citron (for preserving)......	5	.10	100

MELON, Muskmelon—(Cucumis Melo

French, *Melon.* Spanish, *Melon.* German, *Melone.*

	pr pkt.	per oz.	per lb.
Christiana (salmon-colored flesh, round, sweet, netted, extra)	5	.10	1.00
Hackensack Netted (green flesh, round, sweet, very fine) ..	5	.15	1.50
Casaba (long-oval green, netted)	5	.10	1.00
White Japan (round, sweet, extra)	5	.10	1.00
Nutmeg (green-netted, sweet)	5	.10	1.00
Arlington Green Nutmeg, or Cantalenp of some (extra)...	5	.15	1.50
Stickney's Long Yellow Musk (extra)	5	.15	1.50
Large Yellow Musk	5	.10	1.00

MUSTARD—(Sinapis).

French, *Moutarde*.　Spanish, *Mostaza*.　German, *Senf*.

	pr pkt.	per oz.	per lb.
			per qt.
White Seeded	5	.10	.40
Brown Seeded	5	.10	.40

MUSHROOM—(Agaricus Esculentis).

French, *Champignon Comestible*.　Spanish, *Hongo*.
German, *Champignon-Brut*.

	per lb.	per 10 lbs.
English Spawn	.15	1.25

NASTURTIUM—(Tropæolum Majus).

French, *Capucine*.　Spanish, *Capuchina*.
German, *Kresse Indianische*.

	pr pkt.	per oz.	per lb.
Large Pickling	5	.10	1.25

OKRA—(Hibiscus Esculentis).

French, *Gombo*.　Spanish, *Quibombo*.
German, *Essbarrer Hibiscus*.

	pr pkt.	per oz.	per lb.
Dwarf Large Podded (extra)	5	.15	1.50
Tall Long Podded	5	.10	1.00

ONION—(Allium Cepa).　All New England Grown.

French, *Ognon*.　Spanish, *Cebolla*.　German, *Zwiebel*.

	pr pkt.	per oz.	per lb.
Early Flat Red	.10	.40	5.00
Rhode Island Large Red	.10	.40	4.00
Danvers Thick Yellow (Buxton's own, extra, best)	.10	.50	6.00
—— —— ——(choice, fine quality, from Buxton's Stock)	.10	.40	4.50
Yellow Flat	.10	.40	4.50
White Silver Skin (Portugal)	.10	.40	4.50

ONION SETS—Small Onions, for Early crop.
Price Variable.

	per qt.	pr. bu.
White	.50	
Top	.40	
Potato, or Hill Onions	.30	

PARSLEY—(Apium Petroselinum).

French, *Persil*.　Spanish, *Perejil*.　German, *Petersilie*.

	pr pkt.	per oz.	per lb.
Plain-Leaved	5	.10	1.00
Extra Curled	5	.10	1.25
Champion Moss Curled	5	.10	1.25

	pr pkt.	per oz.	per lb

PARSNIP—(Pastinaca Sativa).

French, *Panais*. Spanish, *Pastinaca*. German, *Pastinake*.

	pr pkt.	per oz.	per lb
Early Round Summer	5	.10	1.00
Long Smooth White	5	.10	.60
Student	5	.10	.80
Abbott's Improved	5	.10	.80
Half-Long French	5	.10	.80
Hollow Crown, or Guernsey	5	.10	.80

PEAS. See first page of this List.

PEPPER—(Capsicum).

French, *Piment*. Span. *Pimiento*. Ger. *Spanischer Pfeffer*.

	pr pkt.	per oz.	per lb.
Pickling, Squash or Tomato Shaped	5	.30	4.00
Large Sweet	5	.30	4.00
Large Bell	5	.30	4.00
Cayenne	5	.30	4.00
Red Cherry	5	.40	5.00
Chili (small for Pepper Sauce)	5	.40	5.00

POTATO—(Solanum Tuberosum).

French, *Pomme de Terre*. Spanish, *Batata*.
German, *Kartoffel*.

Best varieties furnished to order in their season.

PRICES ON APPLICATION.

PUMPKIN—(Cucurbita Pepo).

French, *Citrouille*. Spanish, *Calabaza tontanera*.
German, *Kurbiss*.

	pr pkt.	per qt.	pr. bu.
Large Yellow, or Field	5	.25	4.00
Small Yellow Sugar	—	—	—
Mammoth (see Squash).			

PURSLANE—(Portulaca Oleracea).

French, *Pourpier*. Spanish, *Verdolaga*. German, *Portulak*.

	pr pkt.	per oz.	per lb.
Golden (for greens)	5	.15	1.50

RHUBARB—(Rheum Hybridum).

French, *Rhubarbe hybrida*. Spanish, *Ruibarbo hibrida*.
German, *Rhabarber*.

	pr pkt.	per oz.	per lb.
Victoria (fine large)	5	.25	2.50
Linnæus (fine large early)	5	.25	2.50

RADISH—(Raphanus Sativus).

French, *Radis.* Spanish, *Rabanito.* German, *Rettig.*

	pr pkt.	per oz.	per lb.
Early Long Scarlet (selected stock)	5	.10	.60
Wood's Early Frame (scarlet)	5	.10	.80
Early Scarlet Olive-Shaped	5	.10	.80
Early Scarlet Olive-Shaped, White-Tipped (French Breakfast)	5	.10	.80
Early Scarlet Turnip-Rooted	5	.10	.80
White Summer Turnip-Rooted	5	.10	1.00
Yellow Summer Turnip-Rooted	5	.10	1.00
Gray Summer Turnip-Rooted	5	.10	1.00
Black Winter	5	.10	1.00
Chinese Red Winter	5	.10	1.00

RAPE—(Brassica Napus).

	per lb.
Large-Seeded Garden, or Spring Sprouts (for greens)	.20

SALSIFY—(Tragopogon Porrifolius).

French, *Salsifis.* Spanish, *Salsifi.* German, *Haferwurzel.*

	pr pkt.	per oz.	per lb.
Long White (Oyster Plant)	5	.20	2.50

SEA KALE—(Crambe Maritima).

French, *Crambe maritima.* Spanish, *Breton de mar.*
German, *Sel-kohl Meer-kohl.*

	pr pkt.	per oz.	per lb.
Silver Sea Kale	.10	.30	4.00

SORREL—(Rumex Acetosa).

French, *Oseille.* Spanish, *Acedara.* German, *Sauerampfer.*

	pr pkt.	per oz.	per lb.
Large-Leaved French	5	.20	2.00

SQUASH—(Cucurbita Melo-Pepo).

French, *Courge.* Spanish, *Calabaza bonetara.*
German, *Kuchen Kurbiss.*

	pr pkt.	per oz.	per lb.
Early White Scollop	5	.10	.80
Early Yellow Scollop	5	.10	.80
Early Summer Crookneck, or Warted	5	.10	.80
Boston Marrow	5	.10	1.00
Hubbard	5	.10	1.00
Turban (American)	5	.10	1.00
Low's Hard-Shell Turban, or Hybrid	5	.15	1.50
Marblehead (very fine)	5	.10	1.00
Cocoanut (small, sweet, prolific, very fine)	.10	.25	2.50
Canada Crookneck	5	.10	1.00
Large Winter Crookneck	5	.10	1.00
Mammoth Yellow (very large)	.25	.80	
—— French	.10	.40	4.00

SPINACH—(Spinacia Oleracea).

French, *Espinard.* Spanish, *Espinaca.* German, *Spinat.*

	pr pkt.	per oz.	per lb.
Thick-Leaved, Round-Seeded	5	—	.25
Savoy, or Curled-Leaved, Round-Seeded	5	—	.30
Large-Leaved Viroflay, Round-Seeded	5	—	.30
Prickly-Seeded	5	—	.25

TOMATO—(Solanum Lycopersicum).

French, *Tomate.* Spanish, *Tomate.* German, *Liebes-Apfel.*

	pr pkt.	per oz.	per lb.
Early Conqueror (fine early, smooth, bright red)	5	.30	3.00
Acme (pinkish purple, solid flesh, extra)	5	.30	3.00
Paragon (bright red, smooth, very fine)	5	.30	3.00
Hathaway's Excelsior (round, bright red, smooth, extra)	5	.30	3.00
General Grant (smooth, bright red, fine)	5	.30	3.00
Emery (fine early market, extra)	5	.40	4.00
Boston Market (extra early)	5	.40	4.00
Canada Victor (bright red, early)	5	.30	3.00
Trophy (large, very solid)	5	.40	4.00
Early Essex (large, bright red, fine for forcing and market)	5	.40	5.00
Yellow Plum (excellent for preserves)	5	.40	4.00
Fig, or Pear-Shaped	5	.40	4.00
Strawberry or Husk (fine for preserves)	5	.40	4.00

TURNIP—(Brassica Rapa et Napa).

French, *Navet.* Spanish, *Nabo.* German, *Rube.*

	pr pkt.	per oz.	per lb.
Early Snow-Ball	5	.10	.60
Early White Flat	5	.10	.60
Purple Top White Flat	5	.10	.60
Purple Top White Globe	5	.10	.80
White Egg	5	.10	.80
Yellow Stone, or Globe	5	.10	.60
White Pomeranian Globe	5	.10	.60
White Sweet German	5	.10	.60
White French, or Rock	5	.10	.60
London Extra Yellow Swede (fine, oval-shaped)	5	.10	.60·
Shamrock Yellow Swede (globe-shaped, very fine)	5	.10	.60
Carter's Imperial Yellow Swede (globe-shaped)	5	.10	.60
Laing's Swede (globe-shaped, small-leaved)	5	.10	.60
Long White Cow Horn	5	.10	.60
Yellow Aberdeen	5	.10	.60

FLAVORING AND MEDICINAL HERB SEEDS.

	pr pkt.	per oz.	per lb.
Anise (Pimpinella anisum)	5	10	1.00
Arnica (Arnica montana)	.25	2.50	—
Balm (Melissa officinalis)	.10	.40	4.00
Basil, Sweet (Ocymum basilicum)	5	.20	2.50
Borage (Borago officinalis)	5	.15	1.50
Burnet (Poterium sanguisorba)	5	.20	2.00
Belladonna (Atropa Belladonna)	.10	.80	—
Benne (Sesamum orientale)	5	.20	2.00
Catnip (Nepeta cataria)	.10	.40	4.00
Chamomile (Anthemis nobilis)	.10	.50	—
Caraway (Carum carui), for sowing	5	.10	.60
Caraway (Carum carui), for flavoring	—	—	.20
Coriander (Coriandrum sativum), for sowing	5	.10	1.00
Coriander (Coriandrum sativum), for flavoring	—	—	.30
Celery (Apium graveolens)	—	5	.40
Cumin (Cuminum Cyminum)	5	.10	1.00
Dill (Anethum graveolens)	5	.10	1.00
Fennel, Sweet (Fœniculum vulgare)	5	.10	1.00
Horehound (Marrubium vulgare)	.10	.25	2.50
Hyssop (Hysopus officinalis)	.10	.25	2.50
Lavender (Lavendula epica)	5	.15	1.50
Lovage (Levisticum officinalis)	.10	.40	—
Marigold, Pot (Calendula officinalis)	5	.20	2.00
Marjoram, Sweet (Origanum Marjorana)	5	.25	2.50
Pennyroyal (Hedeoma pulegioides)	.15	1.00	—
Rocket (Brassica eruca)	5	.25	2.50
Rosemary (Rosemarinus officinalis)	.10	.40	4.00
Rue (Ruta graveolens)	5	.20	2.00
Sage (Salvia officinalis)	5	.20	2.00
Savory, Summer (Satureia hortensis)	5	.20	2.00
Saffron (Carthamus tinctorius)	5	.20	2.00
Tarragon (Artemesia Dracunculus)	.25	—	—
Thyme (Thymus vulgaris), Broad-Leaved, English	5	.40	4.00
Wormwood (Artemesia absinthium)	5	.25	2.50

USEFUL BOOKS ON GARDENING.

SENT BY MAIL ON RECEIPT OF PRICE.

Money in the Garden (Quinn) $1.50
Gardening for Profit (Henderson) 1.50
Practical Floriculture (Henderson) 1.50
Gardening for Pleasure (Henderson) 1.50
Hand-Book of Plants (Henderson) 3.00

CLOVER SEEDS.

Prices Variable, governed by Market Rates, and Quality.

	W'ght of bushel about	Price about per lb.
Red Northern, or Pea Vine (Trifolium pratense).........	60 lbs	—
—— Western, or Medium (Trifolium pratense)..........	60 lbs	—
Alsike (Trifolium hybridum)	60 lbs	.35
White Dutch (Trifolium repens)	60 lbs	.35
Lucerne, or Alfalfa (Medicago sativa), Imported..........	60 lbs	.40
Lucerne, or Alfalfa (Medicago sativa), American....	60 lbs	.30

GRASS SEEDS.

Prices Variable, governed by Market Rates, and Quality.

	W'ght per bushel about	Price about pr bu.
Timothy (Phleum pratense), extra, best quality	45 lbs	Market prices.
—— —— —— fair medium.....................		
Red Top (Agrostis vulgaris), per sack of about 50 lbs....	10 lbs	
—— —— extra fine heavy seed	14 lbs	1.50
Rhode Island Bent (Agrostis var.).....................	12 lbs	3.50
Kentucky Blue (Poa pratensis) choice clean seed, extra-extra	14 lbs	2.50
Fowl Meadow (Poa serotina), best grass for wet land......	11 lbs	3.50
Orchard (Dactylis glomerata)...........................	14 lbs	2.75
Perennial Rye-Grass (Lolium perenne)................	24 lbs	3.00
Italian Rye-Grass (Lolium Italicum)...................	18 lbs	3.00
Tall Oat-Grass (Avena elatior).......................	12 lbs	3.00

	W'ght	per lb.
Yellow Oat-Grass (Avena flavescens)...	8 lbs	.55
Meadow Fescue (Festuca pratensis)	15 lbs	.10
Tall Fescue (Festuca elatior)	15 lbs	.40
Hard Fescue (Festuca duriuscula)	14 lbs	.30
Sheep's Fescue (Festuca ovina)......................	12 lbs	.30
Meadow Fox-tail (Alopecurus pratensis)	8 lbs	.50
Rough-stalked Meadow (Poa trivialis)	14 lbs	.40
Wood Meadow (Poa nemoralis)	14 lbs	.45
Sweet Vernal (Anthoxanthum odoratum)..	11 lbs	.40
Crested Dog-tail (Cynosurus cristatus).................	28 lbs	.45
Creeping Bent, or Fiorin (Agrostis stolonifera)..........	15 lbs	.25

MILLET SEEDS.

Prices Variable, governed by Market Rates, and Quality.

Very large annual grasses, suitable for green fodder or as a substitute for hay in seasons of scarcity. Seeds can be sown in this latitude from first of June to the middle of July, and on good land from three to four tons of fodder can be grown. They are greatly relished by stock of all kinds, and are especially valuable for milch cows.

	W'ght per bushel about	Price about pr lb.
Hungarian Millet, or Grass (Setaria Germanica).........	48 lbs	Market prices.
Common, or Italian Millet (Setaria Italica).............	50 lbs	
Golden, or German Millet (Setaria var.).................	50 lbs	

GRASS SEEDS FOR LAWNS.

Experience has proved that for various soils and locations, a mixture of grasses is attended with the best results. Our Extra Mixture is composed of the finest and thickest growing sorts, those best adapted to forming a close and permanent sod.

	per qt.	pr. bu.	per lb.
Lawn Grass, Extra Mixture........................	.20	4.00	
Rhode Island Bent Grass. An excellent variety when only one kind of grass is desired	.15	3.50	
Red-Top Grass. Also a good variety to sow alone, though somewhat coarser than the Bent. As it seeds abundantly, it is sold at a much lower price	10	1.50	

White Clover is excellent sown with either of the two last-named grasses, using 2 to 4 pounds to the bushel.

BIRD SEEDS, etc.
Prices Variable.

	per qt.	pr. bu.	per lb.
Canary, Sicily (best quality)	.15		
—— Spanish (best quality)	.15		
—— Smyrna (best quality)	.15	Market prices.	per lb.
Hemp, Russian (best quality)........................	.15		
Rape, English (large-seeded)	.20	4.50	
—— German (small-seeded)	.15	3.00	
Rice, Unhulled..................................	.20	4.00	
Millet	.15	1.75	
—— Large White-Seeded			.12
Mixed Bird Seed	.15	3.00	
Maw (Blue Poppy)			.16
Cuttle Fish Bone ....Per dozen, .20			
Bird Sand	.10		

SEED GRAIN.
Prices Variable.

	per qt.	pr. bu. about	per lb.
Spring Wheat, White Russian......................	.15	3.00	
—— —— Lost Nation	.15	3.00	
Winter Wheat, White Clawson......................	.15	2.50	
Spring Rye			
Winter Rye.....................................			
Barley, Spring, two-rowed		Market prices.	
—— —— four-rowed			
—— —— for fodder crop			
Oats, White Bedford............................			
—— White Probsteier			
Buckwheat......................................	.10	1.00	
—— —— Silver Hull......................	.10	2.00	

FRUIT, HEDGE PLANT AND TREE SEEDS.

Fruit.

	per oz.	per lb.	pr. bu
Apple (Pyrus malus)	.10	.50	
Currant (Ribes)	.40		
Gooseberry (Ribes grossularia)	1.00		
Pear (Pyrus communis)	.25	2.50	
Quince (Cydonia vulgaris)	.25	2.50	
Strawberry (Fragaria)	.80		
Peach (Persica vulgaris), natural fruit			2.50

Hedge.

	per oz.	per lb.	pr. bu.
Arbor Vitæ (Thuja occidentalis)	.40	4.00	
Barberry (Berberis vulgaris)	.15	1.50	
Buckthorn (Rhamnus catharticus), clean	.15	1.50	
Honey Locust (Gleditschia triacanthos)	.10	.75	
Osage Orange (Maclura aurantiaca)	.10	.75	
Privet (Ligustrum vulgare)	.20	2.00	

Tree.

	per oz.	per lb.	pr. bu.
Ash, White (Fraxinus alba)	.20	2.00	
Fir, Norway Spruce (Abies excelsa)	.15	1.50	
—— White Spruce (Abies alba)	.40	4.00	
—— Hemlock Spruce (Abies Canadensis)	.40	4.00	
—— Balsam (Abies balsamea)	.30	3.00	
—— Silver (Abies Pectinata)	.15	1.50	
Larch, European (Larix Europea)	.20	2.00	
Locust, Yellow (Robinia pseudo-acacia)	.10	1.00	
Maple, Sugar (Acer saccharrhinum)	.20	2.00	
Pine, White (Pinus strobus)	.25	2.50	
—— Pitch (Pinus rigida)	.40	4.50	
—— Black Austrian (Pinus nigra Austriaca)	.20	2.00	
—— Scotch (Pinus sylvestris)	.20	2.00	
—— Sea-Side (Pinus maritima)	.15	1.50	

COW PEAS.

We know of no crop for plowing under for green manure that equals this. The seeds are similar to Beans in appearance and growth, and should not be planted until the ground is warm. On good soil that is simply "run out" no manure is required in starting the crop, but on poor land some fertilizer is desirable, though not essential. Repeated crops plowed under will insure a degree of fertility upon any soil not attained by any other green crop we know of. Two bushels of seed per acre, drilled in, is the usual seeding.

Per Quart, 15 cts.; Per Bushel, $2.50.

MISCELLANEOUS SEEDS, etc.

	per qt.	pr. bu.	per lb.
Cotton, Upland, Improved Herlong.			.30
—— Sea Island (long staple)			.20
Broom-Corn Seed (Evergreen)	.20	4.50	
Cow Peas (heavy cropper, for plowing in green)	.15	2.50	
Doura, Branching, White-Seeded Egyptian			.40
Flax Seed		3.50	.10
Sugar Cane (Early Amber)	.30	6.00	
Sunflower	.20	5.00	

	pr pkt.	per oz.	per lb.
Hop Seed	.10	1.00	
Tobacco Seed, Havana	.10	.50	6.00
—— —— Connecticut	.10	.40	4.00

	pr box	per lb.	
Whale Oil Soap, extra best quality, in 2 lb. boxes	.25		
—— —— —— extra best quality, in 5 lb. boxes	.60		
—— —— —— extra best quality, in 10 lb. boxes	1.00		
—— —— —— extra, quantities in firkins or barrels		8	
—— —— —— Chemical Concentrated, in bars, per lb.		.20	
Tobacco Soap (for washing animals or plants)		.40	
Tobacco Dust (for extermination of insects)		.10	
White Hellebore (sure remedy for Currant Worms)		.35	each.
Archangel Mats (for vegetable and plant ties)			75
Raffea (for tying)		.80	
Soft Twine (for tying)		.40	
Grafting-Wax		.30	

EGYPTIAN, OR CHINA CORN (Sorghum Vulgare.)

This is a valuable grain and fodder producing plant, particularly for very hot and dry climates. It will make a crop on poorer land and with less moisture than any other grain. Tested with Indian Corn or Maize, through weeks of dry weather, without rain, the results proved that while the Maize dried up and perished, the Egyptian Corn continued to grow apparently as well as if no drought prevailed. The grain is small and white, matures in about 100 days, and is useful as food for man, animals, and fowls. The yield of grain, usually 75 to 100 bushels per acre, has been known to exceed 150 bushels per acre. As a forage crop it is excellent, either green or dry, and cattle are exceedingly fond of it. It grows 8 to 12 feet high, is very leafy (the Branching variety especially so), and may be cut several times during the growing season. In habit it is similar to Broom Corn, and the culture the same. We offer two varieties:

White-Seeded, Common . . . . per lb., 30 cts.
White-Seeded, Branching, or Rural . . . . " " 40 "

Flower Seeds.

WHAT more can we say in praise of Flowers than others have already done ? Little more, we fear, than to recommend their culture to every person, to the full extent of the time and space they can devote to them. Their brilliant and varied colors eloquently plead their own cause. Their presence gives cheerfulness to home surroundings and renders Parks and Public Grounds more attractive. It is not necessary to grow them largely to derive the greatest pleasure; it is the quantity well cared for, that gives this result. It is often a matter of surprise to note the success attained in their culture by those who have but little time to spare from their other duties. A little time daily works wonders, and it is often noticed that there is more real beauty and attractiveness in a few well-appointed beds *near the house where constantly seen*, than where more is attempted at a greater distance, and not under such constant supervision. We again advise all who can, to cultivate Flowers, and whether on a large scale requiring professional assistance, or on the cottage system in beds near the house, to avoid planting more than can receive proper care, and *that care just at the time when it is needed*. It is not to be expected that within the prescribed limits of a Price-List full directions for the successful culture of Flowers can be given, but a few brief suggestions may be of benefit to beginners and others but partially familiar with the subject, and we therefore offer the following

SUGGESTIONS TO BE REMEMBERED.

Successful culture depends much on various circumstances. While in some locations their culture, owing to the peculiar adaptedness of the soil, climate, and other favorable conditions, is of the simplest character, in others it is quite the reverse, and success is attained only by care, skill, and close observation on the part of the cultivator ; but in this close watching day by day, the true lover of Flowers finds the greatest pleasure, constantly gaining information, and storing up knowledge which, in succeeding years, will render success almost a certainty.

The supposition should not be entertained for a moment that the purchase of a few seeds and the placing of them in the ground, without regard to season, or character of the soil, is all that is necessary to insure an abundance of Flowers.

Those who are not experienced should, as a general rule, confine their selections of varieties to the free growing Annuals, such as Asters, Balsams, Stocks, Petunias, Candytuft, Phlox, Zinnia, etc., and venture but cautiously with varieties requiring delicate culture, until the habits and requirements of such are fully understood.

In the selection of seeds for planting, as it takes as much time and attention to grow Flowers that are poor as those that are good, it is true economy to select the best ; for, the finer and more beautiful the varieties chosen, the greater the pleasure derived in the season of bloom.

A good mellow loam, slightly sandy, is the best for most varieties of Flowers. Soils so sandy that moisture is retained with difficulty, or one that will bake easily soon after being wet, or that is retentive of moisture so as to become sodden, are unsuitable ; but if there is no alternative, and such must be used, then more care becomes necessary in planting the seed, in attention while germinating, and in the after culture of the plants.

Seeds of Flowers are in general small and delicate, many nearly as fine as dust. It can be readily seen how very slender must be the little hair-like sprouts from these diminutive seeds, and how surely they must fail to grow, if roughly planted, or planted in soil as dry as ashes, or in soil coarse and lumpy, or covered an inch or more in depth, or in soil hard underneath, or beat down by rains and firmly crusted on top. A little observation on the part of the cultivator will show how carefully they must be planted, and how gently covered with soil. It is only necessary, with many of these finest, to scatter them on the surface, the ground having been previously made light, and the whole gently and carefully pressed afterwards. If the weather is hot and dry, cover with a light mat until germination takes place. Too early planting in the open ground while it is cold is a prolific source of trouble, and is to be avoided. Seeds thus planted are extremely liable to fail to germinate ; or, should they start, the plants at best grow feebly, linger along, and finally drop off one by one, until another planting becomes necessary, causing much care, loss of time, and with no further advancement than if the planting had been deferred until the soil had become mellow and warm.

If early Flowers are wanted, start the seeds in the house or in a hot-bed, where they can grow until the weather and ground are warm, and then plant them out in the garden ; but care is requisite while in the house or hot-bed, particularly the latter, that the heat is not so great as to injure the seed, or afterwards to burn the plants by failure to give sufficient air.

Beginners in Flower Culture should procure some good and reliable treatise on gardening, to assist them at the outset, and afterwards improve on the information obtained by their own experience.

Flowers are classified as Annuals, Biennials, Perennials, supplemented by varieties requiring Greenhouse culture.

Annuals grow from the seed, bloom, and perish in one season. Some half-hardy varieties of longer duration are classed with Annuals, as they succeed treated as such.

Biennials, from the seed, generally bloom the second year and then die. Some few varieties, if planted early, bloom the first year.

Perennials, from the seed, bloom the second year, and every year thereafter, some perishing after three or four years, while others continue indefinitely.

Seeds of Annuals may generally be expected under favorable conditions, to germinate in ten to twenty days.

Perennial varieties are uncertain, some of the varieties remaining in the ground for a long time before starting into growth. Experiments have proved that some have thus remained for a year from planting, and then come up thickly and made a strong growth. Purchasers of these should not make haste to complain of the quality of the seed, but should make all due allowance for the habits of the varieties.

The following list, which has been prepared with much care, embraces the choicest species and varieties in cultivation —for the most part those that have been thoroughly tested and have proved valuable ; while some varieties of recent introduction, promising well, have been included in the list.

For **Newest** varieties see Special List, page 38, this Catalogue.

FLOWER SEEDS.—GENERAL LIST.

EXPLANATION.—The letters in the following Table explain the *habit* and *duration* of the different varieties.

   a.—annual.
   b.—biennial.
   p.—perennial.
  b. h. p.—perennial, but requiring some protection during winter.
   g.—greenhouse.
   c.—climber.
   e.—everlasting, or eternal (for drying).
  a. p.—perennial, but generally blooms the first year.
 t. g. p.—plants suitable for garden culture in summer, but roots must be kept in
      house or cellar during winter.
   o. f.—ornamental foliage plants.

	per pkt.	per oz.
a Aster, Peony Perfection (Truffaut's).		
—————— package of 12 separate colors $1.00		
—————— " " 8 " " 75		
—————— the same colors mixed	.15	5.00
—— Victoria, Imbricated, Large Flowered		
—————— package of 12 separate colors $1.00		
—————— " " 8 " " 75		
—————— the same colors mixed	.15	5.00
—————— Pure White	.25	6.00
—————— Azure Blue	.25	6.00
—————— Dark Blue	.25	6.00
—————— Carmine Rose	.25	6.00
—————— Dark Crimson	.25	6.00
—— Imbricated Pompon (Truffaut's).		
—————— package of 12 separate colors $1.00		
—————— the same colors mixed	.15	4.00
—————— Pure White	.20	4.00
—————— Rose	.20	5.00
—————— Crimson	.20	5.00
—————— Dark Blue	.20	5.00
—— Pompon Cocardeau. (Asters of the Cocardeau class have beautiful white flowers, with brilliant outside circles of various colors.)		
—————— package of 6 separate colors 1.00		
—————— the same colors mixed	.15	4.00
—— Goliath, Large Flowered.		
—————— package of 6 separate colors 75		
—————— the same colors mixed	.15	
—— Washington, Large Flowered, White	.25	
—————— mixed	.25	

	per pkt.	per oz.

a. **Aster, Large Rose-Flowered.**
———— package of 10 separate colors 75
———— the same colors mixed . . . . | .15 | 4.00
—— **Betteridge's Quilled.**
———— package of 12 separate colors 75
———— the same colors mixed . . . . | .10 | 2.00
—— **Dwarf Chrysanthemum-Flowered**, mixed, 1 ft. | .15 | 5.00
—— **Dwarf Pompon Globe**, mixed, 1 ft. . . . . | .10 | 3.00
—— **Dwarf Bouquet Pyramidal**, mixed, 1 ft. . . . . | .15 | 5.00
—— **Dwarf Shakespeare**, mixed, 1 ft. . . . . | .15 | 5.00
—— **Dwarf Schiller**, mixed, 1 ft. . . . . | .15 | 5.00
—— **Boltze's Bouquet Dwarf**, mixed, ⅔ ft. . . . . . . | .15 | 5.00
—— **Splendid French and German**, extra mixed . . | 15 | 5.00
—— **Quilled and Globe-Flowered**, good mixed . . . | 5 | 1.00
a. **Abronia umbellata**, rose, ½ ft. . . . . | 5 | 1.00
a. p. **Abobra viridiflora**, pretty climber, scarlet fruits, 10 ft. . | .10 | 1.00
a. c. **Acroclinium roseum**, rose, 1 ft. . . . . | 5 | .80
a. c. —— **album**, white, 1 ft. . . . . | 5 | .80
b. c **Adlumia cirrhosa (Mountain Fringe)**, purple, 10 ft. . | .15 | 1.50
a. **Adonis æstivalis**, scarlet, 1 ft. . . . . | 5 | .50
p. —— **vernalis**, yellow, 1 ft. . . . . | 5 | .50
a. **Ageratum Mexicanum**, blue, 2 ft. . . . . | 5 | .80
a. ———— **Imperial Dwarf, Blue**, ⅔ ft. . . . . | .10 | 1.50
a. —— **conspicuum**, white, blooms till frost sets in, 1 ft. . | 5 | .80
a. —— **Lasseauxi**, rose, 1½ ft. . . . . | .10 | 3.00
—— **Agrostemma coronaria (Rose Campion).**
p. ———— **atrosanguinea**, crimson, 2 ft. . . . . | 5 | .80
p. ———— **alba**, white, 2 ft. . . . . | 5 | .80
a. **Amaranthus tricolor**, red, yellow and green foliage, 3 ft. | 5 | .60
a ———— **giganteus**, " " " " " 6 ft. | 5 | 1.00
a. —— **bicolor ruber**, scarlet and orange foliage, 2 ft. . . | 5 | .60
a. —— **melancholicus ruber**, dark, crimson foliage, 3 ft. | 5 | .60
a. —— **atropurpureus**, blood purple foliage, 2 ft. . . . . | 5 | .60
a. —— **salicifolius (willow-leaved)**, scarlet and purple, 3 ft. | .10 | 1.00
a —— **amabilis tricolor**, rose, yellow and fiery red, 3 ft. . | .10 | 1.00
a. —— **Henderi**, dark foliage, 3 ft. . . . . | .10 | 1.50
a. —— **sanguineus elatior**, crimson, 4 ft. . . . . | .10 | 1.00
a. —— **caudatus (Love Lies Bleeding)**, crimson, 3 ft. . . . | 5 | .60
a. —— **finest mixed** . . . . | 5 | .80
a. **Alonsoa linifolia**, scarlet, 1 ft. . . . . | .10 | 1.00
a. —— **myrtifolia**, scarlet, 1 ft. . . . . | .10 | 1.00
a. —— **albiflora**, white, 1 ft. . . . . | .10 | 1.00

	per pkt.	per oz.
a. Alyssum Benthami (Sweet), white, 1 ft.	5	.60
p. —— saxatile compactum, yellow, 1 ft. (Perennial) . .	5	1.00
a.e. Ammobium alatum, everlasting, white, 2 ft.	5	.60
e.p. Ampelopsis Veitchii, hardy climber, 30 ft.	.20	
a.p Anchusa capensis, long blooming, blue flowered, 1½ ft. .	.15	3.00
p. —— italica, blue, 3 ft.	5	.60
e.p. Antennaria margaritacea, white, everlasting, 1½ ft. . .	.15	
g. Angelonia grandiflora, blue flowered pot-plant, 1 ft. .	.25	
p Anemone, mixed, 1 ft.	.10	1.50
a. Anagallis grandiflora, mixed, ¾ ft.	5	2.00
a. Antirrhinum majus, mixed, 2 ft.	5	.80
a. —— —— package of 8 separate colors 50		
a. —— nanum, Dwarf, fine mixed, 1 ft. . . ., ...	5	1.50
p. Arabis Alpina, white, early spring flower, ¾ ft.	.10	2.00
p. Armeria maritima, pink, dwarf edging, ¼ ft.	5	1.50
p. —— Laucheana, red, ¼ ft.	—	—
a. Argemone grandiflora, white, poppy-like flower, 3 ft. .	5	.60
a. —— mexicana, yellow, 1½ ft.	5	.60
Arbutus, see Epigæa repens.		
p. Aquilegia (Columbine), Single, extra fine, mixed, 2 ft.	.10	2.00
p. —— —— Double, finest mixed, 2 ft.	5	.60
p. —— —— chrysantha, yellow, 2 ft.	.15	
p. —— —— cœrulea, blue and white, 2 ft.	.20	
p. —— —— caryophylloides, striped, 2 ft.	.10	
p. —— —— canadensis, scarlet and yellow, 2 ft.	.10	
p. —— —— Skinneri, scarlet and orange, 2 ft.	.15	
a. Asperula azurea setosa, light blue, 1 ft.	5	.50
p. —— —— odorata, white, fragrant, 1 ft.	.10	1.50
p. Asclepias tuberosa, orange, fine, 1½ ft.	.15	
p. Aubrietia græca, rock work and edging plant, purple, ¼ ft.		
Auricula. See Primula.		
a. Balsam, Double, good common mixed, 1½ ft.	5	.60
a —— —— Camellia and Rose-Flowered, Splendid Extra Mixed	.15	3.00
a. —— —— package of 12 separate colors $1.00		
a. —— —— " " 6 " " 60		
a. —— Double, Pure White, 2 ft.	.20	2.00
p. Baptisia australis, blue pea-shaped flower, 2 ft.	5	.75
a. Bartonia aurea, yellow, 1 ft.	5	.00
Balloon Vine. See Cardiospermum.		
a.c. Bean, Scarlet Flowering, rapid climber, 15 ft.	.10	pt. .25
a.c. —— White Flowering, " " 15 ft. . . .	.10	pt. .25

		per pkt.	per oz.
h.h.p.	Bellis Perennis (Daisy), Double, good mixed, ½ ft...	.10	8.00
h.h.p.	—— —— Double, from Prize Flowers, extra mixed	.25	12.00
h.h p.	—— —— Double White, ½ ft..............	.25	12.00
a g.p.	Begonia, Tuberous-rooted Hybrids, finest mixed, 1 ft.	.25	—
o.f.p.	Bocconia Japonica, ornamental foliage plant, 5 ft. ...	.10	1.50
a.g p.	—— frutescens, ornamental greenhouse and lawn plant,	.15	3.00
a.	Brachycome iberidifolia (Swan River Daisy), blue, ½ ft.	5	1.00
a.	Browallia elata, blue, 1½ ft................	.10	1.50
a.	—— —— alba, white, 1½ ft.............	.10	1.50
a.	—— —— fine mixed	.10	1.50
a.	Cacalia coccinea (Tassel Flower), scarlet, 2 ft.	5	.80
a.	Callirhoe pedata nana compacta, dark rose, 1 ft...	.10	2.00
a.	Cannabis gigantea, ornamental foliage, 8 ft.	5	.60
a.	Calandrinia umbellata, rosy crimson, ½ ft.	5	1.50
a.	Calendula (Cape Marigold), Double, mixed, 1 ft...	5	.40
a.	—— officinalis (Pot Marigold), Double, mixed, 1 ft.	5	.60
g.	Calceolaria hybrida grandiflora, from Prize Flowers,	.50	
g.	——.—— —— pumila compacta, finest mixed	.50	
a.g.p.	—— rugosa, fine for summer bedding, mixed, 2 ft. ...	.50	
a.c.	Cardiospermum halicacabum (Balloon Vine), 6 ft. ...	5	.60
a.	Campanula Annual, mixed, 1 ft.............	5	1.00
p.	—— Perennial, Dwarf, mixed, ½ ft...........	5	1.00
p.	—— —— Tall, mixed, 3 ft................	.10	2.00
	—— Medium (Canterbury Bell).		
b.	—— —— Single Rose, 2½ ft.	5	1.25
b.	—— —— " White, 2½ ft.	5	1.00
b.	—— —— " Blue, 2½ ft.	5	1.00
b.	—— —— Single Mixed, 2½ ft.	5	1.00
b.	—— —— Double Mixed, 2½ ft.............	5	1.00
	Canary Bird Vine. See Tropæolum.		
a.g.p.	Canna, ornamental foliage, fine mixed, 4 to 8 ft.	.10	1.00
p.	Catananche cœrulea, blue, 2 ft.	5	.80
g.p.c.	Calampelis scabra, fine orange-flowering climber, 10 ft.	.10	3.00
	Candytuft. See Iberis.		
a.	Celosia cristata (Cockscomb), Dwarf, mixed, 1 ft. .	5	2.00
a.	—— —— Dwarf Crimson, fine strain, 1 ft.......	.15	
a.	—— pyramidalis (feathered), mixed, 3 ft.	5	1.00
a.	—— —— plumosa nana, fine mixed, 2 ft.	.10	2.00
a.	—— Japonica (Japan Cockscomb), scarlet, 2 ft....	.10	1.50
a.	—— Huttoni, dark, ornamental foliage, 2 ft.	.20	
p.	Cedronella cana, purple, fragrant, 2 ft.	.10	1.50
a.	Centranthus macrosiphon, mixed 1½ ft.	5	.60

		per pkt.	per oz.
a.g.p.	Centaurea gymnocarpa, silvery foliage, 1½ ft.	.25	3.00
a.g.p.	—— candidissima, silvery foliage, 1½ ft. . . . 100 seeds	.30	
a.g.p.	—— Clementei, silvery foliage, 1½ ft.	.25	
a.	—— cyanus (Bachelor's Button), mixed, 2 ft.	5	.60
a.	—— moschata (Sweet Sultan), mixed, 2 ft.	5	.60
p.	Chelone barbata, Torreyi, scarlet, 3 ft.	5	1.25
a.	Cheiranthus maritimus (Virginian Stock), mixed, ½ ft	5	.60
a.	Chrysanthemum, Annual, Single, finest mixed, 2 ft.	5	.60
a.	—— Double, finest mixed, 2 ft.	5	.60
g.	—— frutescens (French Marguerite, or Daisy), white .	.25	3.00
h.h.p.	—— Indicum, Pompone, autumn blooming, mixed, 2 ft.	.25	
a.g.p.	Chamæpeuce diacantha, ornamental plant, 1 ft. . . .	.10	
g.	Cineraria hybrida, from Prize Flowers, ex. mixed, 1½ ft. .	.50	
g.	—— Dwarf, splendid mixed, ¾ ft.	.50	
a.g.p	—— maritima candidissima, silvery white foliage, 2 ft.	.10	2.50
a g.p.	—— acanthifolia, silvery foliage, 2 ft.	.15	
a.	Clarkia, Double, fine mixed, ¾ ft.	5	1.00
p.c.	Clematis, fine mixed, 10 ft. (seed starts slowly)	.15	3.00
a.	Clianthus Dampieri, scarlet and black, 2 ft.	.25	
a.	Clintonia, finest mixed, ¼ ft.	.10	3.00
a.	Collinsia, fine mixed, 1 ft.	5	1.00
a. c.	Cobæa scandens, robust climber, purple, 15 ft.	.15	2.50
a.	Convolvulus minor (Dwarf Morning Glory), mixed, 1 ft.	5	.40
g.p.	—— mauritanicus, blue, fine for hanging baskets . . .	.15	2.00
g.	Coleus hybrida, extra fine mixed, 2 ft.	.50	
a.	Cosmea bipinnata, purple, 2 ft.	5	.60
a.	Coreopsis tinctoria, yellow, with brown centre, 2 ft. . . .	5	.60
a.	—— —— nigra, dark red, 2 ft.	5	.60
a.	—— —— Drummondii, yellow and red, 1½ ft.	5	.60
a.	—— —— Annual, finest mixed, 2 ft.	5	
p.	—— Perennial, 3 ft.	5	1.00
a.	Crepis (Hawkweed), red and white mixed, 1 ft.	5	.60
a. c.	Cucumis (Cucumber Gourd), fine mixed, 10 ft.	.10	1.00
a. c.	Cucurbita (Squash Gourd), small sorts, mixed, 10 ft. . . .	.10	1.00
a. c.	—— —— —— large sorts, mixed, 15 ft.	.10	1.00
	Cypress Vine. See Ipomea.		
g. p.	Cyclamen Persicum, choicest Prize Stock, mixed, ¾ ft.	.50	
g. p.	—— —— giganteum, finest mixed, ¾ ft.	.75	
a.g.p.	Dahlia, Large-Flowered, Double, finest mixed, 5 ft.	.25	
a.g.p.	—— Small or Pompone-Flowered, finest mixed, 4 ft.	.25	
	Daisy. See Bellis.		
a.	Datura fastuosa, Double, finest mixed, 4 ft.	.10	1.00
a.	—— humilis, Double, yellow, sweet-scented, 3 ft. . . .	.10	1.00

Delphinium (Larkspur), Annual.

	per pkt.	per oz.
a. ————— — Double Dwarf Rocket, finest mixed, 1 ft.	5	.50
a. ——— —— Double Branching, finest mixed, 2 ft. .	5	.50
a. ——— —— Double Emperor, fine mixed, 1 ft.	5	.80
p. ——— Perennial, Chinese, fine mixed, 2 ft.	5	1.00
p. ——— — formosum, blue, 3 ft.	.10	1.50
p. ——— — nudicaule, scarlet, 1 ft.	.25	
p. ——— — elatum, Single Hybrids, mixed, 4 ft.	5	.80
p. ——— — —— Double Hybrids, finest mixed, 4 ft. . . .	.25	
a. Didiscus cœrulea, blue, 1 ft.	5	1.00
b. Digitalis (Foxglove), finest mixed, 3 ft.	5	.80
p. Dictamnus Fraxinella, red and white, mixed, 2 ft. . . .	.10	1.50
p. Diclytra spectabilis, bright carmine and white, 2 ft. . .	.25	
a. b. Dianthus (Pink), Chinese Double, mixed, 1 ft.	5	.80
a. b. ——— — Hedewigii, Single, fine mixed, 1 ft.	5	1.50
a. b. ——— — " Double White, 1 ft	.10	2.00
a. b. ——— — " Double Dark Red, 1 ft.	.10	2.00
a. b. ——— — " Double fine mixed, 1 ft.	5	1.50
a. b. ——— — Diadematus, Double, extra fine, mixed, 1 ft.	.15	3.00
p. ——— plumarius, Double Hardy Garden, mixed, 1 ft.	.25	
h.h.p. ——— scoticus, Double, Florist's or Paisley, 2 ft. . .	.50	
——— caryophyllus (Double Carnation Pink).		
h.h.p. ——— — —— Dwarf Early, fine mixed, 1 ft.	.15	3.00
h.h.p. ——— — —— Premium Border, selected extra, 2 ft. . .	.25	9.00
h.h.p. ——— — —— Prize Stock, splendid extra mixed, 2 ft. .	.50	
h.h.p. ——— — —— Perpetual, fine mixed, 2 ft.	.50	
h.h.p. ——— — —— Picotee, Prize Stock, finest mixed, 2 ft.	.50	
——— barbatus (Sweet William).		
p. ——— — Single, extra fine mixed, 1½ ft.	5	.80
p. ——— — Single Auricula-Flowered, finest mixed . .	5	1.00
p. ——— — " White, 1½ ft.	.10	1.50
p. ——— — " Scarlet, 1½ ft.	.10	1.50
a. c. Dolichos Lablab, blackish-purple foliage, 8 ft.	5	.40
a. c. Elychrysum (Eternal Flower), Double, mixed, 2 ft. . .	5	1.00
a. c. ——— — package of 10 separate colors 60		
a. c. ——— — bracteatum, Single White, 2 ft.	5	.60
a. c. ——— — " " Yellow, 2 ft.	5	.60
a. c. ——— — Dwarf Scarlet, 1 ft.	5	.60
a. c. ——— minimum, Double, smallest flowered, mixed, 2 ft.	5	.60
a. Erysimum Peroffskianum, orange, 1½ ft.	5	.60
p. ——— pulchellum, dwarf, free blooming yellow, ½ ft. . .	.10	2.00
a. Epigæa (Trailing Arbutus), pink	.15	

	per pkt.	per oz.
a. Eschscholtzia Californica, yellow, 1 ft.	6	.50
a. —— —— alba, white, 1 ft.	6	.50
a. —— —— rosea, rose, 1 ft.	5	.50
a. —— Mandarin, orange and scarlet, 1 ft.	.50	
a. —— Double, fine mixed, 1 ft.	.50	
a. Euphorbia variegata, green, white striped foliage, 2 ft.	5	.60
Feverfew. See Matricaria.		
a. Gaillardia, Annual, fine mixed, 1 ft.	5	1.25
p. —— grandiflora, Perennial, scarlet and yellow, 1½ ft.	5	1.25
t.g.p. Geranium Zonale, fine mixed, 2 ft.	.25	
p. Geum coccineum, Single, scarlet, 2 ft.	5	1.25
p. —— —— Double, scarlet, 2 ft.	.25	
a. Gilia tricolor, mixed, 1 ft.	5	.50
a. —— capitata, white and blue mixed, 1 ft.	5	.50
a.b. Glaucium corniculatum, fine silvery foliage, 1 ft.	.25	
g. Gloxinia hybrida, French, choicest mixed, 1 ft.	.50	
g. —— —— robusta grandiflora erecta, splendid mixed,	.50	
p. Globularia trichosantha, dwarf blue edging plant, ½ ft.	.10	2.50
p.c. Gnaphalium decurrens, everlasting white, 2 ft.	.50	
a. Godetia, Lady Albemarle, crimson, 1 ft.	.10	1.50
a. —— Whitneyi, Brilliant, carmine, edged light rose	.25	
Gourd. See Cucumis and Cucurbita.		
a. Gomphrena globosa (Globe Amaranthus), purple, 2 ft.	5	.80
a. —— —— alba, white, 2 ft.	5	.80
a. —— —— variegata, 2 ft.	5	.80
a. —— —— aurea, orange, 2 ft.	5	.80
a. Gypsophila elegans, white, 1 ft.	5	.60
p. —— paniculata, white, 2 ft.	5	.60
p. —— acutifolia, white, 2 ft.	5	.60
a. Helianthus (Sunflower), Double, Dwarf, 4 ft.	5	.30
a. —— oculatis viridis, Double, yellow, green centre	5	.30
a. —— uniflorus Single, gigantic flowers, yellow, 8 ft.	5	.30
a.g.p. Heliotropium, blue shades, fine mixed, 1½ ft.	.15	4.00
a.g.p. —— Madame de Blonay, white, fine for bouquets	.25	
a.c. Helipterum, Sandfordi, everlasting, yellow, 1 ft.	.10	1.50
p. Hesperis matronalis (Sweet Rocket), mixed, 2 ft.	5	.60
a. Hibiscus Africanus, buff, maroon center, 2 ft.	5	.50
p. Hollyhock, Double German, mixed, 6 ft.	.15	3.00
p. —— —— package of 12 separate colors $1.00		
p. —— Double, from Prize Flowers, finest mixed . . .	.25	
p. —— —— package of 12 separate colors $1.50		
p. —— —— " " 6 " " 75		

	per pkt.	per oz.
a.g.p. Humea elegans purpurea, ornamental plant, 6 ft. . . .	.15	
Honesty. See Lunaria.		
a. Iberis (Candytuft), coronaria, White Rocket, 1 ft. . .	5	.30
a. —— —— odorata, white, sweet-scented, 1 ft.	5	.30
a. —— —— umbellata, Rose, 1 ft.	5	.30
a. —— —— —— Purple, 1 ft.	5	.30
a. —— —— —— Dark Crimson, 1 ft.	5	.30
a. —— —— —— Fine Mixed, 1 ft.	5	.30
p. —— sempervirens (Perennial), white, 1 ft.	.10	2.00
a. Ice Plant (Mesembryanthemum), 1 ft.	5	.60
a. c. Ipomea purpurea (Morning Glory), mixed, 12 ft. .	5	.20
a. c. —— —— package of 10 separate colors 60		
a. c. —— Large-Flowered, extra finest mixed, 12 ft.	.15	1.50
a.c. —— Quamoclit (Cypress Vine), crimson, 10 ft. . . .	5	.60
a. c. —— —— white, 10 ft.	5	.60
a.c. —— —— mixed, 10 ft.	5	.60
a. c. —— —— coccinea, Ivy-Leaved, scarlet, 10 ft.	5	2.00
Jacobæa. See Senecio.		
a. Kaulfussia amelloides, blue, 1 ft.	5	.80
a. —— —— kermesina, crimson, 1 ft.	5	.80
g.p.c. Kennedya, fine mixed, 6 ft.	.25	
a.g.p. Lantana hybrida, finest mixed, 2 ft.	.10	1.25
Lathyrus odoratus (Sweet Pea).		
a. —— —— Finest Selected, Extra Mixed, pr lb. $1.25	5	.15
a. —— —— package of 10 separate colors 50		
a. —— —— White, 4 ft.	.10	.20
a. —— —— Scarlet, 4 ft.	.10	.20
p. —— latifolius (Everlasting Pea), mixed, 5 ft.	.10	1.00
p. Lavendula spica (Lavender), blue, 2 ft.	5	.40
a. Lavatera trimestris, red and white, mixed, 3 ft.	5	.40
Larkspur. See Delphinium.		
a. Leptosiphon hybridus, fine mixed, ½ ft.	.10	1.00
a. Limnanthes Douglasii, yellow and white, fragrant,		
thrives in shady situation, ½ ft.	5	.60
p. Linaria Cymballaria (Coliseum Ivy), for baskets .	.15	
a. Linum grandiflorum (Scarlet Flax), 2 ft.	5	.50
p. —— perenne (Perennial Flax), mixed, 2 ft.	5	1.25
a. Lotus Jacobæus, black-brown and orange, fine, 1 ft. . .	5	1.00
a.g.p. Lophospermum scandens, mixed, 10 ft.	.15	5.00
a. Lupinus, Splendid Varieties, extra mixed, 2 ft. . .	5	.40
a. —— package of 12 varieties, separate 60		
b. Lunaria biennis (Honesty), purple, 2 ft.	5	.60

	per pkt.	per oz.
a.g.p. Lobelia erinus, speciosa, Blue King, dark blue, ¾ ft.	.10	3.00
a.g.p. ——— —— alba maxima, large white, ¾ ft.	.10	3.00
a.g.p. ——— gracilis, blue, 1 ft.	.10	3.00
a.g.p. —— erecta alba, white, ½ ft.	.10	3.00
a.g.p. ——— —— Crystal Palace Compacta, blue, ¼ ft. . .	.15	6.00
a.g.p. —— —— pumila alba, Dwarf white, ¼ ft.	.10	3.00
a.g.p. —— —— kermesina, Dwarf Crimson, ¼ ft. . . .	.10	3.00
a.g.p. ——— —— cœrulea grandiflora, Dwarf Blue, ¼ ft.	.10	3.00
a.g.p. ——— —— Paxtoniana, dark blue and white, ¾ ft.	.10	3.00
p. —— fulgens, Queen Victoria, scarlet, 3 ft.	.25	
a. p. Lychnis fulgens, bright scarlet, 1½ ft.	.10	2.00
p. —— chalcedonica, scarlet, 2 ft.	5	.80
p. —— chalcedonica alba, white, 2 ft.	5	.80
h.h.p. —— Haageana hybrida, various colors, 1½ ft.	.10	1.25
a.g.p. Matricaria (Feverfew), Double White, 1 ft.	.10	3.00
a. Malope grandiflora, red and white, mixed, 2 ft.	5	.40
a. Maize, Japanese Striped, green and white foliage, 6 ft.	5	.15
Marigold. See Tagetes.		
a.g.p Maurandya, finest mixed, 8 ft.	.15	6.00
a.g.p. —— alba, white, 8 ft.	.15	
a.g.p. —— purpurea, purple, 8 ft.	.15	6.00
a.g.p. —— Lacayana, deep rose, or red, 8 ft.	.15	6.00
a. g. Malva miniata, scarlet, 1½ ft.	5	1.00
a. —— crispa, ornamental curled foliage, 6 ft.	5	.60
Mignonette. See Reseda.		
a. Mirabilis Jalapa (Marvel of Peru, Four-o'clocks), mixed,	5	.30
a. —— —— package of 8 separate colors 50		
a. —— longiflora, white, sweet-scented, 2 ft.	.10	.40
a. g. Mimulus cardinalis, scarlet, 1 ft.	.10	3.00
a. g. —— tigrinus, white and yellow ground, spotted crimson,	.15	5.00
a. g. —— —— Double, spotted, ¾ ft.	.15	
a. g. —— moschatus (Musk Plant), yellow, ½ ft.	.15	5.00
Morning Glory. See Ipomœa.		
a. Mimosa pudica (Sensitive Plant), 1½ ft.	5	.80
g. p. Myrsiphyllum asparagoides (Smilax), a graceful climber, invaluable for decorative purposes, 10 ft.	.20	2.00
p. Myosotis (Forget-me-not), mixed, ¾ ft.	.10	3.00
p. —— palustris (true Forget-me-not), blue, ¾ ft.	.15	—
p. —— dissitiflora, dark blue, fine for bedding, ¾ ft. . . .	.15	—
Nasturtium. See Tropæolum.		
a. Nemesia floribunda, white and yellow, fragrant, 1 ft. . .	5	1.00
a. Nemophila, finest mixed, ½ ft.	5	.50

	per pkt.	per oz.
a. Nigella (Love in a Mist), Double, blue and white, 1 ft.	5	.40
a. Nierembergia gracilis, white and violet, ¾ ft.	.10	2.00
a. Nycterinia capensis, white, with yellow centre, ½ ft. . .	.10	2.00
p. Nymphæa (Water Lily), alba, white, 2 ft.	.25	
p. —— " " odorata, white, fragrant, 2 ft.	.25	
p. —— " " cœrulea, blue, 2 ft.	.25	
a.g.p. Nelumbium, " " luteum, yellow, 2 ft.	.50	
g. —— " " rubrum, red, 2 ft.	.75	
a. Nolana, finest mixed, 2 ft.	5	.40
p. Œnothera (Evening Primrose), Dwarf, 1 ft.	5	1.25
p. —— —— Tall, mixed, 3 ft.	5	1.25
a. Oxalis, white, rose and yellow, mixed, ½ ft.	.10	2.25
Papaver (Poppy).		
a. —— Annual, Double, Large-Flowered, mixed, 2 ft.	5	.50
a. —— —— package of 10 separate colors 50		
a. —— —— Double Ranunculus-Flowered, mixed, 1½ ft.	5	.80
a. —— —— umbrosum, Single, scarlet, black spotted . .	.10	4.00
p. —— Perennial bracteatum, scarlet with black centre .	5	.75
p. —— —— orientale, scarlot with black centre, 3 ft. . . .	5	1.25
Pansy (Viola Tricolor), Large-Flowered.		
a.b. —— fine mixed, ¾ ft.	5	2.00
a.b. —— package of 24 separate colors 2.00		
a.b. —— " " 12 " " 1.00		
a.b. —— " " 6 " " 50		
a.b. —— Belgian Blotched, splendid, extra mixed, ¾ ft. . .	.25	6.00
a.b. —— English Prize, from choicest collections, ¾ ft. . . .	.50	12.00
a.b. —— Odier, or Five-Blotched, ¾ ft.	.50	12.00
a.b. —— White, ¾ ft.	.15	
a.b. —— Yellow, ¾ ft.	.15	
a.b. —— Light Blue, ¾ ft.	.15	
a.b. —— Dark Shades (blue and black), finest mixed, ¾ ft.	.15	
a. Petunia, hybrida, single, fine mixed, 2 ft.	5	1.50
a. —— —— White, 2 ft.	.10	2.00
a. —— —— Crimson, 2 ft.	.10	2.00
a. —— —— Small-Flowered, Striped	.15	
a. —— —— Large-Flowered, Striped and Blotched .	.25	
a. —— —— nana compacta (Dwarf Inimitable), 1 ft. . .	.25	
a. —— —— grandiflora, splendid strain, fine mixed ·	.25	
a. —— —— " Fringed, extra mixed	.35	
a. —— —— " Double, extra fine, mixed .	.50	
a. —— —— package of 12 separate colors, Single 1.25		
a. —— —— " " 6 " " Double 75		

	per pkt.	per oz.
a. Palava flexuosa, bright rose with black eye, 2 ft.	.10	1.00
a.g.p. Passiflora (Passion Flower), coerulea, blue, 20 ft. . .	.15	4.00
g.p. —— —— —— coccinea, scarlet, 15 ft.	.25	
p. Pentstemon, extra fine mixed, 2 ft.	.15	6.00
a.o.f. Perilla, atropurpurea laciniata, dark elegant foliage, purplish-black, edges of leaves finely cut, 2 ft.	6	.60
a.g.c. Phaseolus caracalla, fine climber, lilac and white, 10 ft.	.20	
a. Phlox Drummondii, choicest extra mixed, 1 ft.	6	1.00
a. —— —— package of 12 separate colors 1.00		
a. —— —— " 6 " " 50		
a. —— —— Pure White, 1 ft.	.10	1.25
a. —— —— Scarlet, 1 ft. . . . . . ,.	.10	1.25
a. —— —— Dark Crimson, 1 ft.	.10	1.26
a. —— —— Grandiflora, large, brilliant, various colored white-eyed flowers, choicest mixed, 1 ft. . . .	.15	2.00
a. —— —— —— splendens, splendid crimson, white eye . .	.20	2.00
a. —— —— —— package of 8 separate colors 75		
a. —— —— nana compacta (Dwarf), finest mixed	.30	
p. —— decussata (Perennial), newest and choicest, mixed	.15	2.50
p. —— —— nana (Perennial), Dwarf, finest mixed . . .	.50	
a. Portulaca, Single, extra fine mixed, ½ ft.	5	1.00
a. —— —— package of 8 separate colors 50		
a. —— Double, choicest extra mixed, ½ ft.	.15	9.00
a. —— —— package of 8 separate colors 75		
p. Polemonium, blue and white mixed, 1 ft.	6	.50
Primula sinensis (Chinese Primrose), Single.		
g. —— —— fimbriata (fringed), extra mixed, ¾ ft. . .	.50	
g. —— —— globosa alba, white, ¾ ft. . ,.	.50	
g. —— —— " kermesina, crimson, ¾ ft.	.50	
The "globosa" varieties are improved strains with large flowers and of fine compact growth.		
g. —— —— alba, white, ¾ ft.	.50	
g. —— —— atrorubra, dark red, splendid, ¾ ft.	.50	
g. —— —— kermesina splendens, crimson, ¾ ft.	.50	
g. —— —— punctata, spotted, fine, ¾ ft.	.50	
g. —— —— striata, striped, white and carmine, ¾ ft.	.50	
g. —— —— filicifolia (fern-leaved), white, ¾ ft.	.50	
g. —— —— " " " crimson, ¾ ft.	.50	
g. —— —— Double, extra mixed, ¾ ft.	.75	
p. Primula Auricula, choicest mixed, ¾ ft.	.25	
p. —— veris elatior (Polyanthus), fine mixed, ¾ ft. . . .	.10	2.50
h.h.p. —— Japonica (Japan Primrose), finest mixed, 1½ ft. . .	.25	

		per pkt.	per oz.
o.f.p.	**Pyrethrum aureum, Golden Feather,** ¾ ft.	.10	3.00
o.f.p.	——— **Golden Gem,** ¾ ft.	.20	
o.f.p.	——— **laciniatus,** ¾ ft.	.20	
p.	—— **hybridum, Double,** finest mixed, 1½ ft.	.25	
a.	**Reseda odorata (Mignonette),** Large-Flowered	5	.15
a.	——— **Giant Pyramidal,** red, 2 ft.	.10	.75
a.	——— **Bouquet Pyramidal,** red, 1½ ft.	.10	.75
a.	——— **nana compacta (Dwarf),** red, ¾ ft.	.10	.75
a.	——— **Victoria,** crimson scarlet, 1 ft.	.15	—
a.	——— **Hybrid Spiral,** 1 ft.	.15	—
a.	——— **Parsons' White,** 1½ ft.	.10	.75
a.	——— **"Diamond,"** white, 1 ft.	.25	—
a.	——— **Galloway's White,** 1 ft.	.25	—
a. e.	**Rhodanthe maculata,** pretty everlasting, rose, 1 ft.	.10	2.50
a. e.	——— **alba,** white, 1 ft.	.10	2.50
a. e.	—— **atrosanguinea,** crimson, 1 ft.	.15	6.00
o.f.a.	**Ricinus (Castor Bean), sanguineus,** red-leaved, 8 ft.	.10	.30
o.f.a.	—— **borboniensis arborea,** giant plant, with red stems and immense dark green leaves, 15 ft.	.10	.40
o.f.a.	—— **cœrulescens,** bluish green leaves and fruits	.20	—
o.f.a.	—— **Duchess of Edinburgh,** very dark foliage, 8 ft.	.10	.50
o.f.a.	—— **giganteus glaucus,** glaucous green foliage, 8 ft.	.10	.40
o.f.a.	—— **guyanensis nanus,** dwarf, with rose fruits, 4 ft.	.10	.40
	Rocket. See Hesperis.		
a.	**Rudbeckia bicolor,** yellow with black centre, 2 ft.	5	.60
a.	**Salvia coccinea nana compacta,** scarlet, 2 ft.	.10	2.00
a.g.	—— **splendens,** scarlet, 3 ft.	.20	4.00
a.g.	—— **patens,** deep blue, 2 ft.	.25	—
a.g.	—— **farinacea,** early blooming, light blue, 3 ft.	.25	—
o.f.p.	—— **argentea, Perennial,** silvery foliage, 3 ft.	.10	1.00
a.	**Salpiglossis variabilis,** finest mixed	.10	1.50
a.	**Sanvitalia procumbens, Double,** yellow, ¾ ft.	.10	1.00
a.	**Saponaria calabrica,** red and white mixed, ½ ft.	5	.60
a.	**Schizanthus,** finest mixed, 1 ft.	5	.80
	Sensitive. See Mimosa.		
a.	**Senecio elegans (Jacobæa), Double,** mixed, 2 ft.	.10	1.50
a.	**Scabiosa, Dwarf, Double,** finest mixed, ¾ ft.	5	.60
a.	——— —— package of 8 separate colors 50		
a.	—— **Mourning Bride,** black purple and white, 2 ft.	5	.60
a.	—— **atropurpurea major,** mixed, 2 ft.	5	.60
a.	**Silene armeria (Catchfly),** mixed, 2 ft.	5	.60
a.	—— **pendula compacta, Dwarf,** pink, edging, ½ ft.	5	.60

	per pkt.	per oz.

Stock, or 10 Weeks Stock Gillyflower (Mathiola).

		per pkt.	per oz.
a. —— Double Dwarf German, garden saved, mixed . .		5	2.50
a. —— —— —— Large-Flowering, finest pot seed, mixed		.15	6.00
a. —— —— —— —— package of 12 separate colors 1.00			
a. —— —— —— —— " " 8 " " 75			
a. —— —— —— —— Pure White, 1½ ft.		.20	6.00
a. —— —— —— —— Scarlet, 1½ ft.		.20	6.00
a. —— —— —— —— Purple Carmine, 1½ ft.		.20	6.00
a. —— —— —— —— Bright Rose, 1½ ft.		.20	6.00
a. —— —— —— —— Blood Red, 1½ ft.		.20	6.00
a. —— —— —— —— Blue, 1½ ft.		.20	6.00
a.g.p. —— —— Autumnal Brompton, fine mixed, 2 ft. . . .		.20	7.00
a.g.p. —— —— East Lothian Autumnal, finest mixed, 1½ ft.		.25	—
a.g.p. —— —— Perpetual Emperor White, 2 ft.		.25	—
a.g.p. —— —— —— —— White and Crimson, mixed, 2 ft. .		.25	—
a.g.p. —— —— Victoria Brompton (Winter), finest mixed .		.25	—
a. g. Stevia serrata, white, fine for cutting, 2 ft.		.10	3.00
a. g. —— purpurea, purple, 2 ft.		.10	3.00
o.f. a. Solanum robustum, ornamental foliage, 6 ft.		.20	
Smilax. See Myrsiphyllum.			
Sweet Peas. See Lathyrus.			
Sweet William. See Dianthus.			
Tropæolum (Nasturtium), Climbing.			
a. c. —— Large-Flowered, extra mixed, 8 ft.		5	.15
a. c. —— —— —— package of 12 separate colors 75			
a. c. —— —— —— " " 8 " " 50			
a. c. —— —— —— Dark Crimson, 8 ft.		5	.20
a. c. —— —— —— Scarlet, 8 ft.		5	.20
a. c. —— —— —— Yellow, 8 ft.		5	.20
a. c. —— Lobbianum, Climbing		.10	.50
a. c. —— Small-Flowered, extra mixed, 10 ft.		.10	.60
a. c. —— —— —— package of 12 separate colors 75			
a. c. —— Canariense (Canary Creeper), yellow, 12 ft. . .		.10	1.25
a. —— Tom Thumb, Dwarf, extra fine mixed, 1 ft. . . .		.10	.30
a. —— —— —— package of 12 separate colors 75			
a. —— —— —— " " 8 " " 50			
a. —— —— —— Black Crimson King, 1 ft.		.10	.40
a. —— —— —— Scarlet King, 1 ft.		.10	.40
a. —— —— —— Golden King, 1 ft.		.10	.40
a. —— —— —— Ruby King, 1 ft.		.10	.40
a.g.p. Tritoma uvaria (Red-Hot Poker Plant), scarlet, 4 ft.		.10	2.00
a. Trifolium (Sweet Clover), 3 ft.		5	.40

		per pkt.	per oz.
a. Thunbergia, finest mixed, 6 ft.		5	.60
p. Tunica saxifraga, dwarf, red, fine for rock-work, ½ ft.		5	.50
a. Tagetes (Marigold).			
a. —— African, Double, finest mixed, 2 ft.		5	.60
a. —— —— —— package of 6 separate varieties	.40		
a. —— French, Tall, Double, finest extra mixed, 2 ft.		5	.60
a. —— —— —— —— package of 6 separate varieties	.40		
a. —— French Dwarf, Double, finest mixed, 1 ft.		5	.60
a. —— —— —— package of 6 separate varieties	.40		
a —— signata pumila, single dwarf, for masses, 1 ft.		5	.80
a.g.p. Torenia Fournierii, sky-blue, spotted black-purple, ¾ ft.		.25	
a.g.p. —— Baillonii, yellow, with brownish-red throat, ¾ ft.		.25	
a. Valeriana, white and scarlet, mixed, 2 ft.		5	.50
a. Verbena, good common mixed, 1 ft.		5	1.50
a. —— hybrida, Extra Mixed, from named flowers, 1 ft.		.15	5.00
a. —— —— candidissima, White, 1 ft.		.25	
a. —— —— —— Light Blue, 1 ft.		.25	
a. —— —— —— Black Blue, 1 ft.		.25	
a. —— —— Scarlet, 1 ft.		.25	
g.p. —— Citriodora (Aloysia), lemon-scented, 2 ft.		.25	
a. Veronica, Annual Sorts, mixed, 2 ft.		5	1.50
p. —— Perennial sorts, mixed, 3 ft.		5	1.50
p. —— candida, dwarf, sky-blue, silvery foliage, fine, 1 ft.		.10	2.00
a.g.p. Vinca rosea, rose, 2 ft.		.10	2.00
a.g.p. —— alba, pure white, 2 ft.		.10	2.00
a.g.p. —— alba oculata, white with red eye, 2 ft.		.10	2.00
a. Viscar a, finest mixed, 1 ft.		5	.60
p. Viola (Violet), fine mixed, ½ ft.		.15	2.50
p. —— —— Italica (Italian Forcing), blue, ½ ft.		.15	
p. —— odorata semperflorens, sweet-scented, ½ ft.		.15	2.50
a.g.p. Wallflower (Cheiranthus), Double, fine mixed, 2 ft.		.20	8.00
a.e. Waitzia grandiflora, everlasting, yellow, 1 ft.		.15	
a. Whitlavia grandiflora, fine mixed, 1 ft.		5	.40
g.o.f. Wigandia caracasana, fine large-leaved plant, 6 ft.		.25	
g.o.f. —— imperialis, splendid variety, 6 ft.		.25	
a.e. Xeranthemum (Everlasting) Double White, 2 ft.		5	1.00
a.e. —— —— Double Purple, 2 ft.		5	1.00
a. Zinnia elegans, Double, extra fine mixed, 3 ft.		5	1.00
a. —— —— —— —— package of 8 separate colors	.60		
a. —— Haageana, Double, orange, 1 ft.		.15	
a. —— Darwini, Dwarf, Double, finest mixed, 1½ ft.		.15	

SPECIAL LIST

OF

FLOWER SEEDS.

This list comprises recently introduced varieties, some quite new, and others older, of which brief descriptions are given.

Amphicarpœa monoica. A tuberous-rooted papilionaceous hardy climber, as powerful a grower as the Scarlet Runner, and as pretty in flower as Kennedyas, $0.25

Calendula Officinalis "Meteor." New splendid variety of the Pot Marigold, with very large and beautifully imbricated, extremely double striped flowers, the colors being of a bright deep orange on a pale straw-colored, almost white ground. A showy and profuse bloomer, and particularly well adapted for bedding purposes 15

Candytuft. New Carmine. A very beautiful variety, of dwarf compact habit of growth, and free-blooming. The flowers are bright carmine, and when grown in masses present a most brilliant appearance 10

☞ **Chrysanthemum frutescens "Etoile d'Or."** A new golden yellow variety of the lovely French Marguerite, so much admired, and useful for cut flowers. Forces well in Greenhouse 25

Chrysanthemum frutescens. The "White Marguerite" of the French, much prized for the cut blooms in the winter. Known also as "White Paris Daisy." Forces well in Greenhouse .26

☞ **Celosia cristata "Empress."** A new giant sort of Cockscomb, producing very large purple-crimson combs, and dark foliage. A beautiful variety. Annual 25

Coleus. Splendid new hybrids of this most elegant plant 50

Cyclamen Grandiflorum. This variety represents the finest strain of Cyclamen in cultivation. The flowers are remarkable for their unusual large size, great substance, finish and form of petals, and their unique brilliancy and attractive coloring. Three named varieties:

     Picturatum, white ground suffused with pink, claret base ⎱ The
     Rosy Morn, clear, bright, delicate rose . . . . ⎰ collection   2.25
     Duke of Connaught, rich purplish crimson . . . . . .

The above three varieties, mixed, per packet 1.00

Dahlia Coccinea. New mixed colors of the now so popular small flowered single variety 25

Dianthus Heddewigii. "Eastern Queen." Large flowers, beautifully marbled, and having broad bands of rich mauve upon the surface of the petals. Striking and pretty. Biennial 15

Dianthus Heddewigii. "Crimson Belle." As its name implies, this variety is of a rich, vivid, crimson-lake color; flowers very large and of good substance. Biennial 15

☞ Eschscholtzia. "Rose Cardinal." A new and lovely variety, with soft, clear, rosy-carmine flowers, the delicate tint extending to the interior as well as the outside of the flower. Annual 30

Eschscholtzia. Californica Alba Flore Pleno. From the Double Golden Yellow variety we now have this fine Double White variety, which will, no doubt, prove an acquisition. Annual 25

Gnaphalium Leontopodium (Edelweiss). This is the true Edelweiss of the Alps, so much prized by tourists in Switzerland. The plant is dwarf; flowers pure white, star-shaped and downy. Perennial 30

Gnaphalium decurrens. A perennial, forming a dense, compact, branching bush, about twelve inches high, out of which rise numerous heads of white flowers in dense clusters. It can be treated as an annual, as it comes to perfection the first season when sown early. The neat globular flowers are sure to become great favorites amongst Everlastings, being more elegant than Antennaria, used so extensively at present — while, at same time, the plant is of easy growth . .50

☞ Larkspur. Double Stock Flowered "Lustrous Carmine." An entirely new color of the Annual Branching Larkspur, far surpassing in beauty most of the colors heretofore obtained. It is of a fiery or lustrous carmine and very brilliant 30

Lobelia Erinus Grandiflora Duplex atrocœrulea. A new double form of the large-flowering Lobelia, reproducing itself quite constant from seed; of much longer duration of bloom than the single varieties 15

Lobelia pumila cœrulea grandiflora. Large blue-flowered, very dwarf variety 15

☞ Marvel of Peru, Dwarf Pure White. A Tom Thumb variety, of nine or ten inches in height, forming a charming compact little bush, studded with snow-white flowers. Comes very true from seed, and is specially adapted for the formation of masses and ribbon borders. Annual 50

Marigold French "Cloth of Gold." A charming variety of striped Marigold, obtained by many years of careful selection. In height, eighteen inches; of free blooming habit, and the petals distinctly marked with bright gold bars, on dark velvet ground. It is recommended as an acquisition 15

Mentzelia Ornata. One of the grandest new introductions from California, noble foliage and stately white flowers. Annual 25

Megarrhiza californica. A new, very rapid growing cucurbitacea of elegant habit and handsome appearance, very rapid in growth, attaining a length of twenty to thirty feet in one season. The leaves have a beautiful silvery gloss, flowers small, in slender racemes, while the oblong-shaped fruits, about two inches long, are densely covered with stout spines similar to those of Echinocystis lobata. The plant develops fully, grown as an annual, but can be cultivated as a perennial, as it produces long and large tuberous roots . . . . . **Large Seeds — each** .15

Molucella Lævis (Shell Flower). An old plant, but comparatively little known. Its singular habit and curiously formed shells are quite attractive, and it should always have a place among the novelties of the Flower Garden. Annual 15

Pansy, Bugnot's Paris International. A superb strain, comprising the most beautiful of the magnificent varieties exhibited by Mr. Bugnot, a celebrated cultivator, on the grounds of the late Paris Exhibition 50

Pansy. "Snow Queen." A new variety, recommended as reproducing itself very true from seed. Its color is a delicate satiny-white, with a tinge of yellow in the centre. A very useful and desirable variety for bouquet work or bedding . . .25

Papaver Umbrosum. A new annual Poppy, growing one and a half feet high. The flowers are of intense brilliant crimson, with a shining black spot on each petal; very showy 15

Petunia Hybrida Robusta Flore Pleno. A new, most distinct, and remarkable novelty, of very compact and symmetrical growth. The flowers are both *smooth* and *fringed-petaled*, of the most beautiful shades, and are so freely produced that a fully developed plant has all the semblance of an artificially made bouquet 50

Petunia Grandiflora Fimbriata Fl. Pl. A magnificent large double *fringed* variety, of exquisite form and coloring, rivaling in delicacy and richness of tints the finest carnations 50

Petunia Grandiflora, Single Fringed. A beautiful variety, with large flowers finely fringed 50

Petunia Hybrida, New Dwarf Inimitable. A new dwarf variety, each plant forming a compact and densely-branched bush, five to eight inches high by as much in diameter, and a remarkably profuse bloomer. The flowers begin to open when the plants are but three inches high, and are of a brilliant cherry-red, each one marked with a regularly formed white star 30

Primula Sinensis Fimbriata "Vesuvius." A magnificent Primula. The rich brilliant crimson-scarlet flowers are of immense size, elegantly fringed and of great substance. Superb 1.26

Primula Sinensis Umbellata Alba. A fine new, robust growing Primula, very floriferous, and produced in umbels 50

Primula Sinensis Cristata Nana Alba. This is a highly interesting and distinct French race. The plant is of a dwarf and dense habit of growth, with foliage crimped or curled like Malva Crispa. Its charming flowers, of snow-white with a pale yellow eye, are acutely dentated and show a tendency to become double 50

Pyrethrum Aureum Selaginoides. The flat foliage of this charming new and distinct variety resembles two fronds of a species of Fern, overlaying each other; a peculiarity which gives to the dwarf and compact plant a particularly fine and even appearance. The fact of its not flowering the first year, is a great recommendation, as the constant pinching back so necessary with the variety P. Aureum, is entirely obviated. It cannot fail to become a most popular variety 50

Reseda Odorata, Golden Queen. An attractive and distinct variety of Mignonette, of dense pyramidal habit of growth. It throws up very numerous flower-stalks, terminated by spikes of golden yellow blossoms, which, with the bright green foliage of the plant, forms a pleasing contrast 25

Reseda Odorata, Galloway's White. A true white variety of Mignonette, recommended as the best pure white yet introduced 26

Salvia Farinacea. This will doubtless become a general favorite. The plants from early sown seed begin to bloom as early as July, the flowers of a light blue on erect spikes nine to eighteen inches long, and not only the flowers, but the wooly-haired bracts, colored from light to dark blue, which keep on for months, constitute a large portion of the beauty of the plant. One of the showiest and most useful blue-flowering Annuals 25

Stock, Ten Weeks, New Giant Perfection. Splendid race of pyramidal growth, with long spikes of beautiful large double flowers. Height two and one half feet. Very fine for open ground culture. White and crimson mixed 25

Sunflower. "Oscar Wilde." The famous Newport Corsage Sunflower. An entirely distinct variety, which originated at Newport, R. I. During last season at this noted watering-place, hundreds were worn daily by the ladies as Corsage Flowers. The plant is dwarf and pyramidal in form, flowers are small, with jet black centre surrounded with an overlapping row of broad, deep, golden yellow petals, and are produced in the greatest abundance from June until killed by frost. .25

Viola Odorata, Munbyana. A fine novelty among violets, recommended as hardy, very free blooming, and excellent for edging 25

☞ **Tropæolum, Tom Thumb "Empress of India."** This new variety is of dwarf, compact habit, like "King of Tom Thumbs," with dark tinted foliage, and flowers of deep brilliant crimson, but much deeper and richer than in the variety just named. A valuable addition to the *King of Tom Thumb* varieties. Annual 35

Xeranthemum Annuum Superbissimum. A new globe-flowered, very double variety, by far the best Xeranthemum hitherto known, which will be found indispensable for all who make use of dried flowers.

     Double White 25
     Double Rose 25

ORNAMENTAL GRASSES.

FOR WINTER BOUQUETS AND ORNAMENTAL GARDENING.

B, for bouquets.   *S*, garden specimen plants.

			per pkt.
a. B.	**Agrostis nebulosa,** elegant, fine, and feathery, 1½ ft.	$ 5
a. B.	—— **pulchella,** exceedingly graceful, 1 ft.	5
a. B.	**Avena sterilis** (Animated Oats), drooping spikes, 2 ft.	5
a. B.	**Briza Maxima** (Quaking Grass), pretty shaking panicles, 1½ ft.	5
a. B.	—— **minima,** small, graceful variety of above, 1 ft.	5
p. B.	**Bromus brizæformis,** elegant, drooping panicles, 2 ft.	5
a. B.	**Chrysurus aureus,** pretty bouquet grass, 1 ft.	5
g. p. S.	**Erianthus Ravennæ,** fine free growing, large variety, 8 ft.	.15
a. B.	**Eragrostis elegans** (Love Grass), useful, elegant variety, 2 ft	5
a. S.	—— **maxima,** very handsome and decorative variety, 4 ft.	.15
a. B.	—— **ægyptiaca,** elegant silvery white inflorescence, 2 ft.	5
a. B.	—— **pilosa,** elegant blackish infloresence, 1 ft.	5
p. S.	**Eulalia Japonica,** elegant variety, 5 ft.	.20
g. p. S.	**Gynerium argenteum (Pampas),** silvery plumes, 8 ft.	.20
g. p. S.	—— **jubatum (Pampas),** silvery plumes, 6 ft.	.20
a. B.	**Lagurus ovatus** (Hare's-Tail Grass), white silky plumes, 1 ft.	5
p. B.	**Melica ciliata,** splendid bouquet grass, 2 ft.	.10
p. B.	**Stipa elegantissima,** most elegant and graceful variety, 1 ft.	.10
p. B.	—— **pennata** (Feather-Grass), beautiful feathery plumes, 1½ ft.	.10
p. B.	**Tricholæna violacea,** elegant, fine rosy-violet tinted, 2 ft.	.10

FLOWER SEEDS

IN PACKAGES OF ASSORTED VARIETIES.

THE following packages will be found desirable for purchasers wishing assortments of Flower Seeds, particularly those who do not care to select for themselves.

We use only popular and choice sorts, and best in quality, in these packages.

Assortment **A** . . . . . 10 varieties of choice **Annuals** . . . . $ .50
      "   **B** 10   "   "   " **Perennials** 50
      "   **C** 25   "   "   " **Annuals** 1.25
      "   **D** 25   "   "   " **Perennials** 1.25

Other assortments, large or small, furnished if desired, consisting of either Annuals or Perennials, or both, to suit the purchaser; also, assortments of rare and choice varieties, for Greenhouse or Garden culture.

COLLECTIONS OF CHOICE VARIETIES

OF

FRENCH AND GERMAN FLOWER SEEDS

IN PACKAGES OF SEPARATE COLORS.

THESE collections consist of packages of seeds as imported, of special varieties of the same flower, each package containing from four to twelve different colors, each separate. Where the greatest variety of colors of *special* Flowers is desired, these collections are invaluable. All these collections are included, each under its appropriate head, in the preceding general list of Flower Seeds, but are here arranged in tabular form for the greater convenience of purchasers of these collections only.

Aster, 12 colors, Truffaut's Peony Perfection $1.25
—— 8 " " " " 75
—— 12 " Victoria Imbricated Large-Flowered 1.25
—— 6 " " " " " 75
—— 12 " Truffaut's Imbricated Pompon 1.00
—— 6 " Crown Pompon Cocardeau 50
—— 6 " Goliath 75
—— 10 " Large Rose-Flowered 75
—— 12 " Betteridge's Quilled 75
—— 12 " German Quilled 50
—— 12 " Pyramidal Globe-Flowered 50
—— 12 " Dwarf Chrysanthemum-Flowered 1.00
Balsam, 12 colors, Camellia-Flowered, Double 1.00
—— 6 " " " " 60
—— 8 " Carnation-Striped, Double 75
Stock, 12 colors, Large-Flowering Dwarf Double German, ten weeks 1.00
—— 8 " " " " " " " " .75
Antirrhinum (Snapdragon), 8 colors, splendid varieties 50
Canna, 12 varieties 75
Celosia (Cockscomb), 6 colors, Dwarf 50
Delphinium (Larkspur), 10 colors, Double Rocket 50
—— " 8 " Double Branching 50
Dianthus Caryophyllus (Double Carnation Pink), 12 varieties 1.25
Dianthus Chinensis, 12 colors, Double 60
Eternals (Elichrysum), 10 colors .50
—— " 8 " Double 50
Everlasting (Immortelles), 25 varieties 1.50
Gourds, 12 varieties, Ornamental 60
—— 12 " " Smallest Sorts 60
Grasses, Ornamental, 12 varieties 75
—— 24 " 1.25

Hollyhock, 12 colors, Double German $1.00
————   12 "   Prize Double 1.50
————   6 "   "   "   .75
Ipomea (Morning Glory), 10 colors, annual climber 60
Lathyrus Odoratus (Sweet Pea), 10 colors 50
Lobelia, 10 varieties 75
Lupinus, 12 varieties 60
Mirabilis hybrida, 8 colors (Marvel of Peru, Four-o'clocks) 50
Pansy, 24 varieties 2.00
————   12   " 1.00
————   6   " 50
Papaver (Poppy), 10 colors, Double, annual 50
Petunia, 12 colors, Single 1.25
————   12 "   Double 1.50
————   6 "   " 75
Phlox, 12 colors, Drummond's Annual 1.00
————   6 "   "   " 50
————   6 "   "   "   Grandiflora 75
Portulaca, 8 colors, Double 75
————   8 "   Single 50
Primula Sinensis, 12 varieties (Chinese Primrose) 2.00
Ricinus, 10 varieties (Castor Bean) 1.00
Salpiglossis, 8 colors 60
Scabiosa, 8 colors, Double Dwarf 50
Tagetes (Marigold), 6 varieties, Double African 40
———— ——   "   6   "   Double French, Tall 40
———— ——   "   6   "   "   "   Dwarf 40
Tropæolum (Nasturtium), 12 colors, Large-Flowered, Climbing 40
———— ——   8 colors "   "   "   "   . . : .50
———— ——   12 colors, Lobbianum, Small-Flowered, Climbing 75
———— ——   12 "   Tom Thumb, Dwarf 75
———— ——   8 "   "   "   " 50
Verbena hybrida, 6 colors 75
Zinnia, 8 colors, Double 60
————   6 "   Dwarf 60

BULBOUS AND TUBEROUS ROOTS.

(FOR SPRING PLANTING.)

GLADIOLUS.—Splendid French Hybrids.

Of summer blooming plants, for general garden decoration, the Gladiolus is deserving of special attention. Requiring but little room for growth, they are exceedingly useful for filling up vacant places in the borders; while for massing in large beds, where a brilliant and effective display is desired, they are invaluable. The splendid French Hybrids are conceded by critical florists to excel all others in diversity and richness of coloring, as also in beauty and form of flowers. We offer true French grown roots of our own importation, in *mixtures of colors*; in *mixtures of special shades*; and in *named varieties of special colors.*

IN MIXTURES.

	Each.	Doz.	Hund.
Extra Fine Mixed, French, Imported. All Colors	10	.75	$5.00
Mixed, Common, for cheap planting	5	.50	3.50

IN SHADES.

	Each.	Doz.	Hund.
Rose and Violet Shades, Extra Fine Mixed	12	$1.00	—
Scarlet and Red Shades, Extra Fine Mixed	12	1.00	—
White Shades, Extra Fine Mixed	12	1.00	—
Yellow Shades, Extra Fine Mixed	12	1.25	—

NAMED VARIETIES IN COLLECTIONS.

Any of the varieties may be had separately, if desired.

CLASS NO. 1. Twelve Varieties, Choice Flowers, Fine Colors.

Addison, dark amaranth, lightly striped with white	$ .40
Etendard, white, purple throat	.35
Eldorado, yellow, crimson throat	.25
Lamarck, bright fiery-scarlet, white throat	.25
Madame Furtado, rosy-white, striped and blazed carmine	.25
Martha, white, blazed with carmine-rose	.35
Pericles, bright rose-flamed carmine, white throat	.35
Racine, brilliant cherry-carmine, white throat	.30
Romulus, brilliant dark crimson, white throat	.20
Stella, light yellow, stained and spotted with carmine	.25
Themis, delicate satin-rose flushed carmine, creamy throat	.30
Thunberg, bright orange scarlet, white throat	.25

The above Class of twelve, one root of each, $3.00. $3.50

CLASS NO. 2. Twelve Varieties, Extra Flowers, Superb Colors.

Amalthee, pure white, occasionally spotted crimson, violet-red throat	$ .50
Antigone, deep rose, flamed carmine	.50
Celimene, bright salmon, flamed crimson	.75
Colbert, vivid carmine-crimson, white lines	.25
Eugene Scribe, very delicate rose, blazed and edged carmine	.40
Galilee, brilliant fiery-red, flamed crimson	.30
Margarita, white ground, suffused and flaked carmine	.25
Meyerbeer, brilliant vermilion-red, purple throat	.25
Milton, white, tinted and flaked rose and crimson	.50
Regina, white, with delicate tint of lilac	.40
Rosea Perfecta, very clear rose with light centre, white lines	.40
Schiller, beautiful buff, rich carmine throat	.50

The above Class of twelve, one root of each, $4.50. $5.00
The two Classes, 24 roots in all, one root of each, $7.00.

GLADIOLUS. SPLENDID FRENCH HYBRIDS.

The following magnificent varieties, taken either together or separately, are worthy a place in any collection, however choice and select it may be. For richness of coloring and form of flowers, they are pre-eminently beautiful, and quite unsurpassed.

Ambroise Verschaffelt, rosy-carmine, flamed with garnet . . . . $ .75
African, dark brown on scarlet ground, white throat 1.50
De Mirbel, bright rosy-pink, with tint of carmine 1.25
Diamant, fleshy white, striped carmine, white throat 1.25
Horace Vernet, brilliant carmine, deeply tinted vermilion, white throat 1.25
Jupiter, light red, shading to dark crimson, with blackish tint 1.25
Le Tintoret, fine rosy-cherry, flamed-carmine, carmine blotched 50
Lemoinei, creamy white and purple crimson, bordered with yellow 1.00
Le Vesuve, splendid spike, fine dazzling scarlet of the greatest brilliancy 1.25
Mary Stuart, white, tinged and blazed with bright carmine cherry 75
Marie Lemoine, pale cream and salmon-lilac, spotted violet and bordered with yellow, 1.00
Matador, brilliant carmine red, striped and blotched with pure white 1.00
Madame Krelage, rosy-ground, flaked crimson 1.25
Orpheus, light ground, blazed with carmine, purple throat 1.00
Reine Blanche, fine clear white, dark carmine throat 1.00

TUBEROSE.

A tender bulbous plant of the easiest culture, suitable for the summer garden, or for house forcing throughout the year. For gardens in warm latitudes they may be planted in spring, when danger of frost is past, in good soil, well enriched with fine old cow manure or rich compost, setting the bulbs six to ten inches apart and slightly under the surface. Where the growing season is short, they must be started in pots in the house, and afterwards turned out into the borders when the weather is settled and warm. The bloom commences in twelve to fourteen weeks from planting, and usually consists of fifteen to thirty flowers, which are pure white and very fragrant.

	Each.	Doz.	Hund.
Double Dwarf, Pearl, splendid variety, extra flowering bulbs . . 10	$1.00	$6.00
Double Dwarf, Pearl, good flowering bulbs 8	.75	5.00

DAHLIA.

Of summer flowering plants the Dahlia is one of the best, and justly termed the glory of the autumn garden. Being tender, the planting should be deferred until the weather has become settled and warm in spring, and the roots taken up before frosts set in, in autumn. One shoot only should be allowed to a plant, and each plant should be supported by a stout stake during the growing season. The varieties are divided into three classes. The "*Show*" and "*Fancy*" are large-flowering, and the plants vary in height from three to six feet. The "*Bouquet,*" "*Lilliputian,*" or "*Pompon,*" have very small flowers, and are suitable for bouquets, hence the name. They are often very erroneously termed "*Dwarf,*" which leads at times to much disappointment, as the plants vary from three to six or more feet in height. *Dwarf* Dahlias are distinct from either of the preceding, and are scarce and not easily obtained. The flowers are as large as the Show varieties, but the plants are very stocky and short-jointed, and seldom exceed two or two and a half feet in height. Of this class (strictly true) there are as yet but very few colors.

	Each.	Doz.
Show and Fancy, Double, choice colors, assorted 15	$1.50
Bouquet, Lilliputian, or Pompon 15	1.50
Dwarf, or Tom Thumb, Large-Flowering 15	1.50

MADEIRA VINE.

A tuberous-rooted climbing plant of rapid growth, with beautiful, thick, wax-like light green leaves, and fragrant, feathery, white flowers. Its culture is simple; the root needs but to be planted and a trellis or strings given it to climb upon. The root is tender and somewhat like a potato, and may receive the same treatment, as respects frosts, housing, etc.

	Each.	Doz.
Selected Roots 10	.75

NOYES' ·HAND WEEDER.

This is one of the best implements ever invented for assisting where HAND WEEDING is required — light, safe, and remarkably easy to use. Two patterns are manufactured; one diamond-shaped, with pointed end, the other with a square end for working in very narrow rows, where the height of the plant necessitates a drawing stroke.

Price, 35 cents each. Per dozen, $3.50.

EXCELSIOR WEEDER.

A very useful implement for eradicating weeds when first starting into growth, but more especially useful (in our experience) for loosening the soil in borders.and beds where a larger tool could not be used.

Price, 25 cents.

FIRE-FLY HAND PLOW.

This is another extremely useful little implement. Every person having a garden to care for (*particularly those too small to admit of horse culture*), should own one. The moldboard is made of steel, wearing bright and clean, and makes as perfect work for its size as an ordinary plow. With it ground can be wholly and thoroughly turned over, or furrows for planting made, and for after weeding it can be most successfully used, turning the furrows outward at one time and inward the next, and so on. Having thoroughly tested one ourselves, we are free to say that the quality of the work done by this little tool is surprising.

Price, $4.00.

RUHLMAN'S HAND CULTIVATOR.

NOTE. — *A*. The cast-steel Knife, corrugated so as to be set at any angle required. *C*. Thumb-screw to raise or lower the handle. *D*. Ridged brace for supporting and regulating the handles *E*. Thumb-screw for regulating blade shanks.

This Hoe, or Cultivator, is a most valuable addition to Garden Implements, and without doubt the best Garden Weeder in use. It is especially adapted to the culture of all garden crops that require careful hand cultivation, and particularly for gardens where horse culture cannot be allowed. It is easily regulated by set screws as to the depth of cutting, the pitch of the knife blades, and height of handles. It is easily worked, and does its work with a thoroughness that will satisfy all who try it.

The frame and wheel are made of the best cast iron. The knives are the best cast steel. They can be set to work 7 to 16 inches in width. They cut the weeds only on the inside of the knife, so that any person can walk along within an inch of, and without injury to, the smallest or tenderest plant, which no other Cultivator can do. It will do the work of six men with common hoes. Reports from those who have given it a trial run in this manner: "It is a promising tool" "It is the best Hoe I ever used." "This is the best Hoe in use." "It will pay for itself in one day." We have no doubt that such will be the universal opinion of all who try it. **Price, $5.50.**

PLANT STAKES (Round).

5 ft. long × 5/8 in. dia.

4 ft. × 9/16 in. "

3 1/2 ft. × 9/16 in. "

3 ft. × 1/2 in.   "

2 1/2 ft. × 7/16 in. ·

2 ft. × 3/8 in. ·

1 1/2 ft. × 5/16 in ·

THE

CHASE

PATTERN.

The best made, for House, Greenhouse, Conservatory, and LIGHT garden work, where plants require support.   Being round, turned tapering their entire length, and painted green, they are exceedingly neat, rather ornamental than otherwise, and in use are not unpleasantly conspicuous.

				Less than 10 of a Size.	In larger quantities.
1½ feet (round, painted)				. 2 cents each	. $1.50 per hundred.
2 "	"	"		. 2 " "	. 2.00 " "
2½ "	"	"		. 3 " "	. 2.50 " "
3 "	"	"		. 4 " "	. 3.50 " "
3½ "	"	"		. 5 " "	. 4.50 " "
4 "	"	"		. 6 " "	. 5.00 " "
5 "	"	"		. 7 " "	. 6.00 " "
6 "	"	"	(Dahlia)	. 14 " "	. 12.00 " "

PLANT STAKES (Square, or Nourse Pattern).

These are larger and possessed of greater stiffness than the preceding sort, and consequently are better adapted for heavier work, and for the support of plants of robust growth.

			Less than 10 of a Size.	In larger quantities.
2 feet (painted)			. 2 cents each	. $2.00 per hundred.
2½ "	"		. 3 " "	. 2.50 " "
3 "	"		. 4 " "	. 3.50 " "
4 "	"		. 6 " "	. 5.00 " "
5 "	"		. 7 " "	. 6.00 " "
6 "	"	light	. 9 " "	. 8.00 " "
6 "	"	extra heavy (Dahlia)	. 18 " "	. 16.00 " "

WOOD POT LABELS.

		Per hundred	Per thousand
4 inch		per hundred, 25 cents.	Per thousand, $1.00
5 "		" " 25 cents.	" " 1.25
6 "		" " 25 cents.	" " 1.50
3½ " Tree		" " 25 cents.	" " 1.00
12 " by 1¼ in. wide, for garden plants		" " 75 cents.	

WHALE OIL SOAP.

One of the most effective, simple and cheapest preparations for the preservation of Trees, Plants, Shrubs, Vines, Rose Bushes, and House and Garden Plants in general, from the ravages of Slugs, Worms, and the various other Insects that infest them. It is sold in the form of thick soap, to be diluted with water as required for use, quite weak for *tender* plants, and stronger according as the hardiness of the plants will permit. For Trees, applied to the foliage, it may be stronger than for small plants, and for cleansing their trunks from Bark-Lice, Worms, and Moss, it may be used of the consistency of common whitewash, and is best applied with a whitewash brush, with syringe to aid in penetrating where the brush fails to reach. As a general rule for application to foliage, seven gallons of water to one pound of soap may be used; but for safety the proper proportion is best ascertained by first mixing the solution, and then testing its strength before using, by immersing a single twig or branch of the kind of plants to which it is to be applied, and wait a few hours for the result. If too strong, more water should be added. If too weak, gradually add more soap until strong enough to kill the Insects without injuring the plants.

Put up in neat boxes (labeled, with directions for use, etc.) containing 5 lbs.; 10 lbs.; and in larger packages, boxes and barrels, to order.

Also, smaller quantities than 5 lbs. sold in concentrated form in Bars.

For Price, see page 21.

TIN SYRINGES for applying the solution, $1.00.

GRAFTING WAX.

This Wax is made for us by an experienced nurseryman, who has used large quantities of it, and finds it to give excellent satisfaction. It is neatly put up in one-quarter, one-half, and one pound packages.

Price per Pound, 30 cents.

POWDERED WHITE HELLEBORE.

The Hellebore Powder has proved the quickest and most efficacious agent thus far employed for the destruction of the Currant Worm. Although in nature poisonous, it is used with perfect safety for the purpose here recommended. It may be sifted on to the worms through a fine sieve, or better if applied with bellows made for the purpose.

Price per Pound, 35 cents.

FRENCH BELLOWS, for applying (*their cost saved in one season*), $2.25.

POT PLANT FERTILIZER.

Flower Food, prepared especially for House Plants, we keep constantly in stock. While a powerful agent, it is inodorous, and no inconvenience is experienced by its use. It is neatly put up in convenient packages, labeled with directions for use.

Price, 25 to 50 cents.

CARBOLIC PURIFYING POWDER.

This Powder, recommended by physicians and scientific men, and adopted by Boards of Health in some of the most prominent cities, acts like magic in removing all disagreeable and unhealthy odors. It is the best disinfectant known, and far more pleasant and effective than Chloride of Lime. It is invaluable for Sinks, Drains, Water Closets, Damp and Mouldy places, and, in fact, to use on all kinds of offal, or in places where bad odors exist. It is a preventive of Fevers, promotes the health and vigor of animals, and will free them from vermin if applied thoroughly. It will protect Poultry from disease and lice by giving them enough to roll in. It may be safely used around the roots of Trees, Vines and Plants, to save them from the ravages of worms and insects. It is cheap and should be in general use everywhere.

Put up in neat Boxes with perforated top and cover for ready use. Price, 25 cents.